VACATION BIBLE SCHOOL ACTIVITIES
For ages 7-12

by Dee Leone
illustrated by
Darcy Tom

Cover by Kathryn Hyndman

Shining Star Publications, Copyright © 1990
A Division of Good Apple, Inc.

ISBN No. 086653-525-X

Standardized Subject Code TA ac

Printing No. 987654321

Shining Star Publications
A Division of Good Apple, Inc.
1204 Buchanan, Box 299
Carthage, IL 62321-0299

Unless otherwise indicated, the King James Version of the Bible was used in preparing the activities in this book.

DEDICATION

This book is dedicated to all my former students,
with wishes for a summer full of joy and special blessings.
Special thanks to my husband,
Joe,
for all his help and encouragement.

SS1818

TABLE OF CONTENTS

Shining Star Publications, Copyright © 1990, A division of Good Apple, Inc.
SS1818

Shining Star Publications, Copyright © 1990, A division of Good Apple, Inc.

SS1818

A WORD TO TEACHERS AND PARENTS

This book has been divided into six sections: memory verses, crafts, songs, snacks, games, and a special carnival section. Use them to instill in each child a joy and appreciation for summer!

The memory verse section contains manipulatives and other reproducibles to help children remember special verses. To use these pages, first make a copy. Then write the verse on the copy, rather than the original. Reproduce the copy with the verse. In this way, the original can be used over and over again with different verses.

The craft section contains a variety of projects, most of which require easily obtainable materials. Most of the craft pages and the memory verse pages can be photocopied on regular paper, but will be more durable if produced on the heaviest paper possible. One way to do this is to use a thermafax machine to make a spirit master of the pattern. The spirit master can then be placed on a mimeograph machine and copied on construction paper or other heavy paper.

The song section contains new songs sung to old familiar tunes. They are great for sing-a-longs. Add them to your collection of favorite home or Vacation Bible School songs.

The snacks in this book are simple enough to be made by the children. They can also be prepared ahead of time by parents or teachers.

The games include both activity sheet games (which also can be used as work sheets) and outdoor games. Additional games, for use at any time, can be found in the carnival section.

A great culminating activity for the last day of Vacation Bible School (or for backyard fun) is to put on a carnival with biblical themes. This can be a service project, a fund raiser, or simply a fun day. Suggestions and games can be found in the carnival section of this book.

Use a different page for each day of summer vacation or choose specific daily or weekly themes. Nine themes, with corresponding ideas, are suggested below, but the possibilities are endless. A carnival can be held on the last day after all the themes have been covered.

THEME 1—FOOD AND FRIENDSHIP
Study the Lord's Supper, the Loaves and Fish, Jesus and the Children, the Manna in the Desert, or any other reference to food or friendship. Use getting acquainted activities for making new friends. Have a picnic and play a friendly game of sports (suggested pages: 10, 12, 18, 20, 28, 31, 34, 37, 62, 63, 66, 72, and 74).

THEME 2—SUNSHINE AND JOY
Study the miracles of healing, with emphasis on blindness and light. Discuss the beatitudes or any reference to light or happiness (suggested pages: 17, 24, 26, 35, 36, 38, 41, 52, 56, and 63).

THEME 3—GOD'S CREATURES
Study creation, Noah's Ark, the Shepherd and His sheep, individuality, etc. (suggested pages: 14, 30, 42, 43, 60, 64, 69, 76, 77, 88, 90, and 95).

THEME 4—SAND, STICKS, AND STONES
Study David and Goliath, the stone tablets with the Ten Commandments, Exodus, casting the first stone, building on a solid foundation, Peter and the church, etc. (suggested pages: 8, 44, 46, 47, 51 and 91).

THEME 5—WONDERFUL WATER
Some Bible stories to cover are the changing of water into wine at Cana, calming the sea, walking on water, the parting of the Red Sea, and the Baptism of Jesus. Tell children the day before to wear clothes they won't mind getting wet. Then take them outside for some water fun (suggested pages: 6, 14, 25, 49, 68, 81, 89, and 95).

THEME 6—GOD'S GLORIOUS GARDEN
Study Adam and Eve in the Garden, the parables of the mustard seed and the sower, the lilies of the field, etc. (suggested pages: 7, 11, 32, 33, 40, 54, 55, 60, 61, 70, and 84).

THEME 7—KALEIDOSCOPE OF COLOR
Read about Joseph's coat of many colors, the rainbow after the flood, and any biblical reference to color (suggested pages: 16, 26, 39, 53, 62, 68, 82, and 94).

THEME 8—TRAVELING INTO BIBLICAL TIMES
Almost any Old or New Testament story could be covered (suggested pages: 18, 57, 65, 67, 77, 78, 80, and 87).

THEME 9—OF KINGDOMS AND TREASURES
Study the Kingdom parables, the story of Solomon's wisdom and riches, the story of the rich man, the meaning of giving, etc. (suggested pages: 8, 62, 83, and 92).

MEMORY VERSES
BIBLE VERSE MEMORY "ADE"

These visual "ades" are a refreshing way to get children to learn Bible verses. One ade already contains a memory verse. Write a verse on the other glass of lemonade before reproducing. Try to reproduce the page onto tagboard or heavy construction paper, if possible. You may want to use several verses and display several glasses of verse lemonade (with or without spinning wedges) on a bulletin board.

MATERIALS:

Lemonade patterns
Two paper fasteners
Crayons or markers
Scissors

DIRECTIONS:

1. Color and cut out the pieces.
2. Carefully cut along the dotted lines of the loose lemon wedges and remove those sections.
3. Punch a hole in the center of all the lemon wedges.
4. Use a paper fastener to attach each loose lemon wedge to a glass.
5. Turn the lemon "window" clockwise as you study parts of each verse.

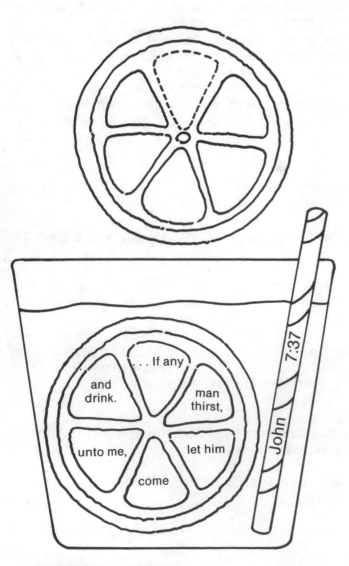

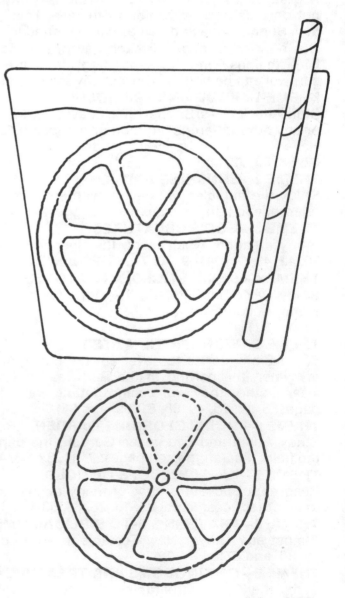

POSSIBLE VERSE:

". . . he that believeth on me shall never thirst."

John 6:35

  SS1818

MEMORY VERSE LEI

Use these flowers to form a beautiful summer lei.

MATERIALS:

Flower patterns reproduced on heavy paper
Yarn
Crayons
Scissors
Pencil
Paper punch (optional)

DIRECTIONS:

1. Color and cut out each flower. Write a part of a memory verse on the back of each flower.
2. Punch or cut a small hole in each flower.
3. Cut a piece of yarn long enough to hang around your neck.
4. String the flowers in the order of the memory verse and tie around your neck.
5. Practice the verse one flower at a time.

POSSIBLE VERSES:

"Now there are diversities of gifts, but the same Spirit."   I Corinthians 12:4

"Behold, how good and how pleasant it is for brethren to dwell together in unity!"

Psalm 133:1

Shining Star Publications, Copyright © 1990, A division of Good Apple, Inc.   SS1818

MEMORY VERSE SAND CASTLE

Children can open these numbered castle "windows" in order to learn a new memory verse. On the copy of the bucket page, write the book, chapter, and verse number of the verse you wish the children to memorize. Within the solid lines on the copy of this page, write the verse, a few words at a time, in the numbered spaces and reproduce.

MATERIALS:

Sand castle patterns
Crayons
Scissors
Glue

DIRECTIONS:

1. Color and cut out the pieces.
2. Cut along the dotted lines of the castle windows and doors.
3. Fold back along the remaining side of each window and door.
4. Cover the verse page with glue, except for the sections containing the words.
5. Glue the castle on top of the verse page. Make sure windows and doors are lined up accordingly.
6. Open the windows and doors in numbered order as you practice your verse.

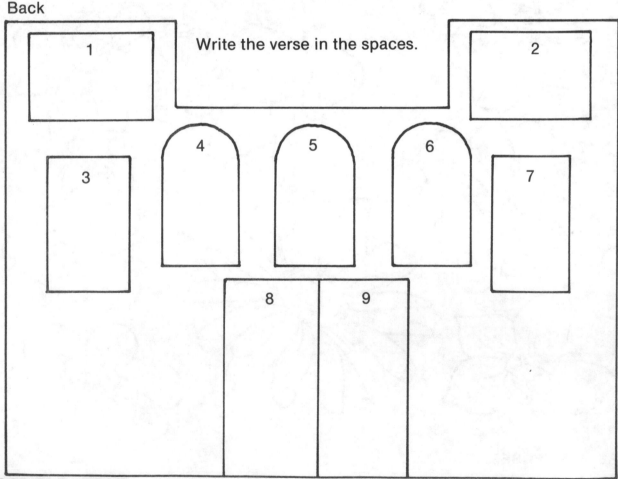

Back

Write the verse in the spaces.

1 2 3 4 5 6 7 8 9

POSSIBLE VERSE:

"Verily I say unto you, Whosoever shall not receive the kingdom of God as a little child shall in no wise enter therein."
Luke 18:17

  SS1818

Front

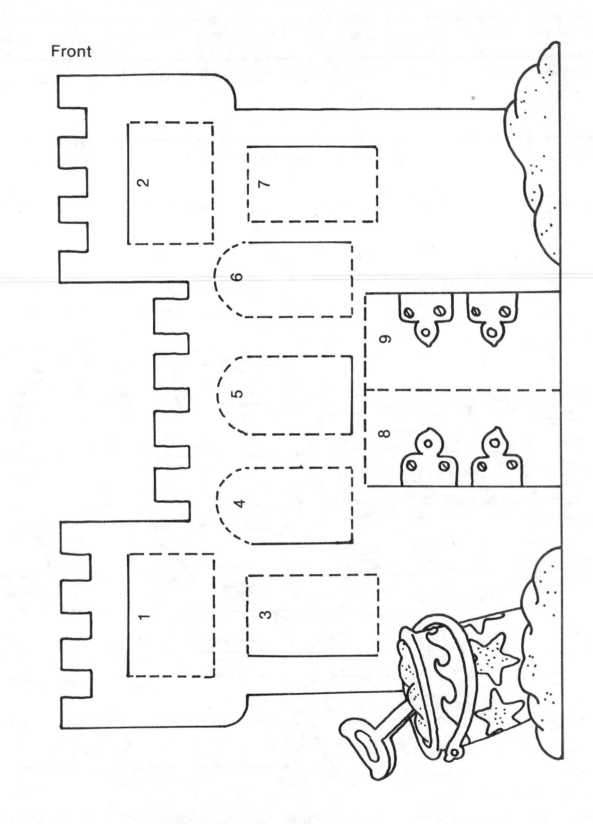

 SS1818

SUMMER SANDWICHES

Children can learn a few verse words at a time as they open these sandwiches layer by layer. One sandwich already contains a memory verse. Any memory verse desired can be written from top to bottom on the other sandwich before reproducing.

MATERIALS:

Sandwich patterns
Crayons or markers
Scissors

DIRECTIONS:

1. Color and cut out the sandwiches.
2. Fold along the dotted lines accordian style.
3. Open one fold at a time as you practice the verses.

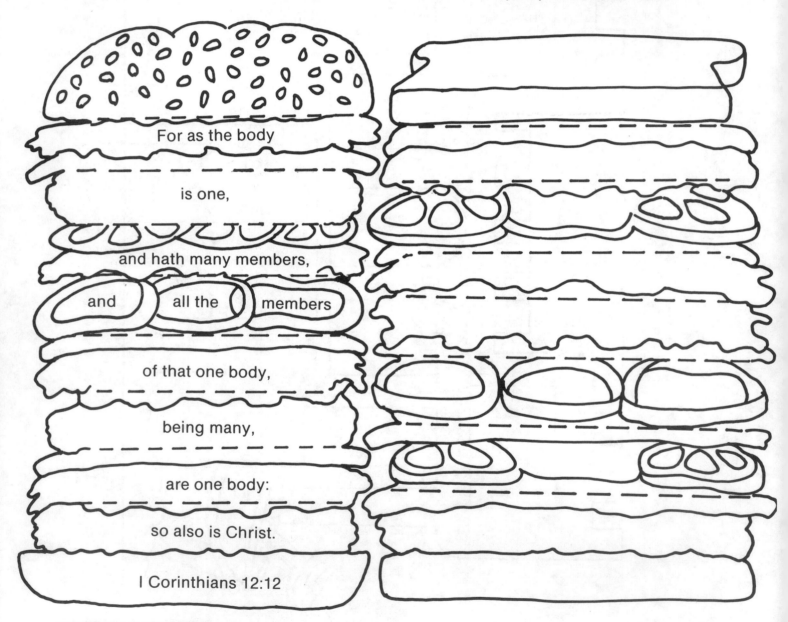

For as the body

is one,

and hath many members,

and   all the   members

of that one body,

being many,

are one body:

so also is Christ.

I Corinthians 12:12

POSSIBLE VERSES:

". . .we, being many, are one body in Christ, and every one members one of another."

Romans 12:5

". . .we being many are one bread, and one body: for we are all partakers of that one bread."

I Corinthians 10:17

SS1818

THE FRUIT OF THE SPIRIT

Memorize the fruit of the spirit with the help of this summertime fruit.

MATERIALS:

Watermelon patterns
Crayons or markers
Scissors
Glue

DIRECTIONS:

1. Color and cut out the watermelon slices.
2. Carefully cut along the dotted lines and fold back the remaining side of each "window."
3. Put glue on the watermelon slice which does not contain seeds. Do not put any glue on or close to the squares containing the words.
4. Carefully set the watermelon with seeds on top of the slice with glue.
5. Open the windows to help you memorize the words of the verse.

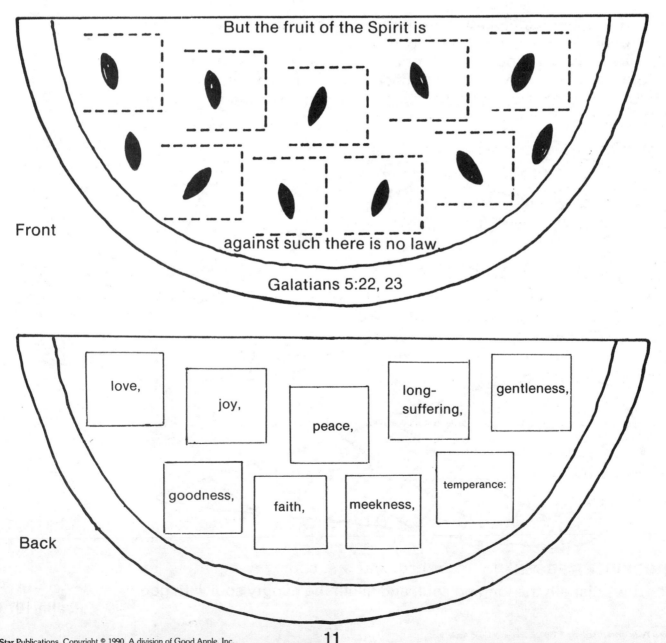

Front

But the fruit of the Spirit is

against such there is no law.

Galatians 5:22, 23

Back

love,
joy,
peace,
long-suffering,
gentleness,
goodness,
faith,
meekness,
temperance:

TASTE AND SEE THE GOODNESS OF THE LORD

Children can learn a verse a few words at a time as they open these ice cream scoops layer by layer. One ice cream concoction already contains a memory verse. Any memory verse desired can be written from bottom to top on the other ice cream scoops before reproducing. Write the verse reference on the bottom scoop.

MATERIALS:

Ice cream patterns reproduced on heavy paper
Scissors
Scrap construction paper
Crayons or markers
Glue

DIRECTIONS:

1. Color and cover each scoop differently by adding chocolate chips, nuts, fruit, etc., made out of construction paper scraps. Be careful not to cover the words of the verse.
2. Cut out the cones and the entire set of scoops. Be sure not to cut off any single scoops.
3. Glue a bottom scoop to each one.
4. Start at the top layer and fold back each scoop one at a time along the dotted lines.
5. "Unroll" one scoop at a time to learn the memory verse.

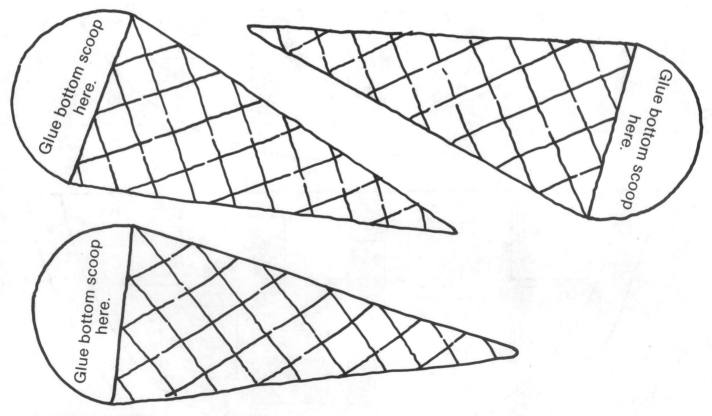

POSSIBLE VERSE:

". . .he satisfieth the longing soul, and filleth the hungry soul with goodness."

Psalm 107:9

SS1818

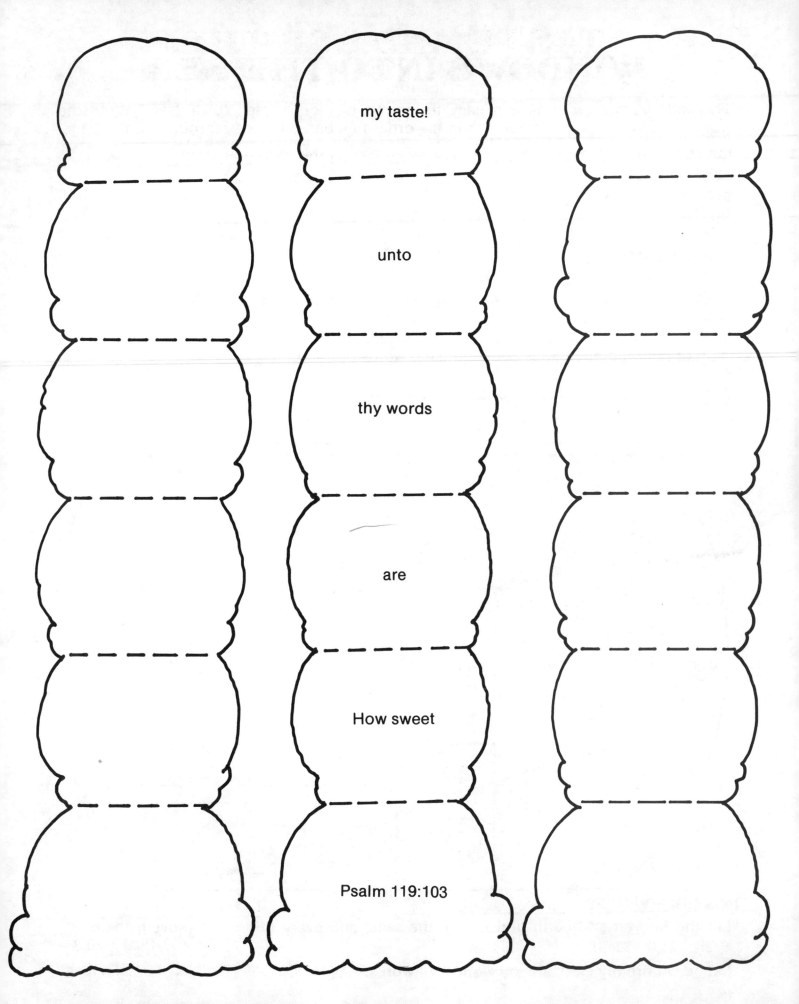

my taste!

unto

thy words

are

How sweet

Psalm 119:103

SS1818

WINDOWS INTO THE SEA

This manipulative will make it easy to learn a memory verse. You'll "sea." Write the words to a verse in the rectangles in the order numbered before reproducing the page.

MATERIALS:

Sea patterns
Crayons or markers
Scissors
Glue

DIRECTIONS:

1. Color the sea picture.
2. Cut out the materials. Also, cut along the dotted lines of the sea picture.
3. Fold back the remaining side of each "window."
4. Put glue on the page containing the verse, but make sure you do not put any glue in or near the rectangles containing the words of the verse.
5. Set the sea picture on top of the glue.
6. Open the windows one by one to learn the memory verse.

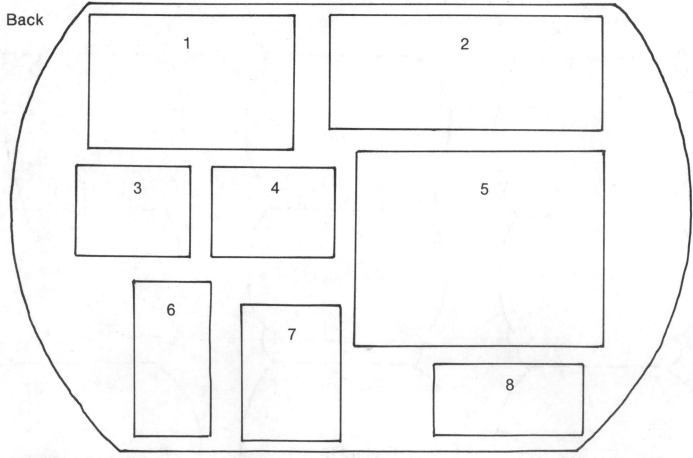

POSSIBLE VERSES:

"Let the heaven and earth praise him, the seas, and every thing that moveth therein."

Psalm 69:34

"Many, O Lord my God, are thy wonderful works. . . ."

Psalm 40:5

SS1818

Front

15

SS1818

LIFE-SAVING VERSES

You can write verses on these "life preservers" before reproducing or you can have children write the verses on afterwards. Let them study the verses until they are "preserved" in their minds. You may even want to make a bulletin board of colorful "life-saving" verses.

MATERIALS:

Patterns reproduced on paper of several colors (or white paper)
Pencil
Scissors
Markers or crayons

DIRECTIONS:

1. Cut out one inner tube of each color. Other children can use the remaining inner tubes. Color the inner tubes various colors if they are on plain white paper.
2. Write a verse on each one (unless it has already been done) and memorize it.

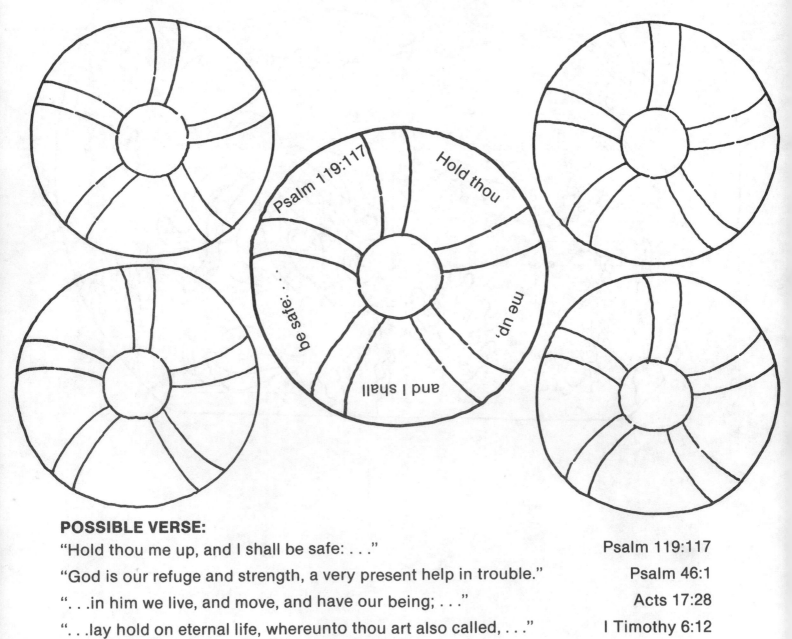

POSSIBLE VERSE:

"Hold thou me up, and I shall be safe: . . ."   Psalm 119:117

"God is our refuge and strength, a very present help in trouble."   Psalm 46:1

". . .in him we live, and move, and have our being; . . ."   Acts 17:28

". . .lay hold on eternal life, whereunto thou art also called, . . ."   I Timothy 6:12

BEACONS OF LIGHT

Summer is a good time to discuss the biblical theme of light. Read and discuss verses with the themes of light, hope, God's protection, etc. Have children write verses to go along with these themes on the lighthouse rays. An option is to enlarge the pattern, write verses on it, and use it as a bulletin board.

MATERIALS:
Pattern
Crayons or markers
Pencil

DIRECTIONS:
1. Write a verse you want to remember on the lighthouse rays.
2. Color the lighthouse.

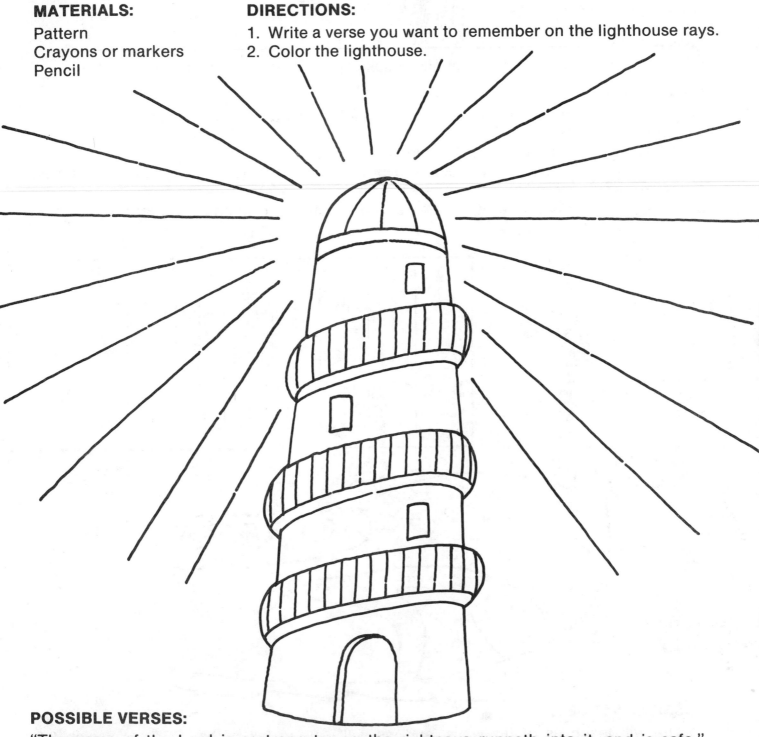

POSSIBLE VERSES:

"The name of the Lord is a strong tower: the righteous runneth into it, and is safe."
Proverbs 18:10

"I am come a light into the world, that whosoever believeth on me should not abide in darkness."
John 12:46

Shining Star Publications, Copyright © 1990, A division of Good Apple, Inc. SS1818

WALK IN LOVE

Before reproducing these memory verse manipulatives, write the book, chapter, and verse number of a verse you need to remember on the top of the sock. Write the verse words from top to bottom on the sock lines. Reproduce on heavy paper, if possible.

MATERIALS:

Girl or boy shoe and sock patterns
Crayons or markers
Scissors
Odds and ends such as glitter, sequins, stickers, bows, and paper scraps (optional)

DIRECTIONS:

1. Color and decorate the shoe and the sock with fancy designs, glitter, stickers, etc.
2. Cut out the sock and the shoe.
3. Cut along the dotted lines of the shoe.
4. Fold back the tabs on the sock and unfold them again once the sock is inserted into the shoe.
5. Lift up the sock a little at a time as you practice the memory verse written on it.

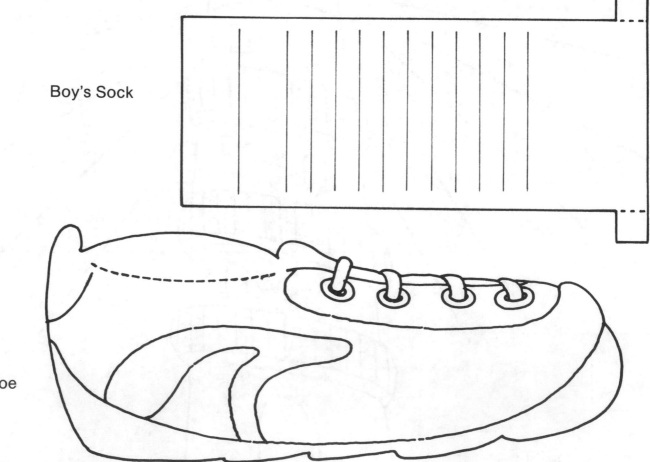

Boy's Sock

Boy's Shoe

POSSIBLE VERSES:

". . .he will teach us of his ways, and we will walk in his paths: . . ."   Isaiah 2:3

"As ye have therefore received Christ Jesus the Lord, so walk ye in him:"   Colossians 2:6

"If we live in the Spirit, let us also walk in the Spirit."   Galatians 5:25

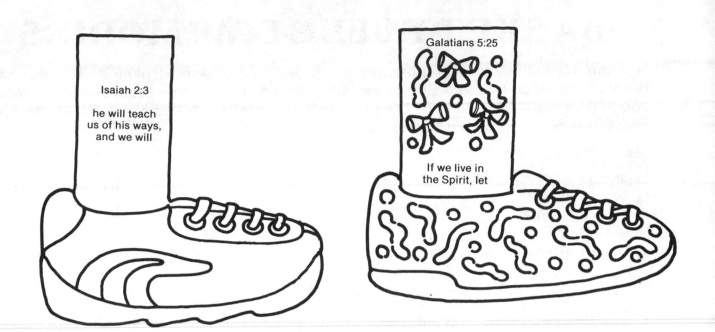

Isaiah 2:3

he will teach us of his ways, and we will

Galatians 5:25

If we live in the Spirit, let

Girl's Sock

Girl's Shoe

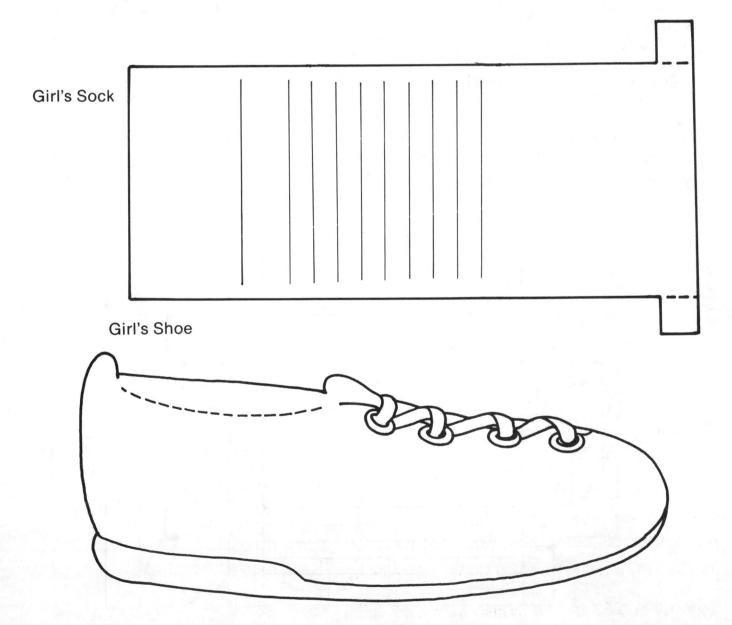

BASKET FULL OF MEMORIES

Use this basket to store the memory verse pieces on the next page and/or the game pieces from "Picnic Pairs." Before reproducing the copies, write the words of a memory verse in order on the rolls of bread from the largest to the smallest. Write the book, chapter, and verse number on the basket handle.

MATERIALS:

Basket and bread patterns reproduced on heavy paper
Glue
Crayons or markers
Scissors
Tagboard (optional)

DIRECTIONS:

1. Color the basket and the breads.
2. Cut them out. (You may want to make the pieces sturdier by gluing them to tagboard or construction paper before cutting, if the patterns have been produced on regular paper.)
3. Fold back along the heavy solid lines.
4. Put glue on the basket tabs and glue the tabs which are numbered the same together.
5. Glue the end of the basket handles to the handle tabs.
6. Arrange the rolls of bread on a pile in order of size. The largest roll should be at the top covering the smaller ones.
7. Look at the word on the top roll. Try to say the next word of the verse before lifting the first bread roll. Whenever you make a mistake, start over. Soon you will be able to make it through the entire pile of bread rolls and you will have learned a new verse.

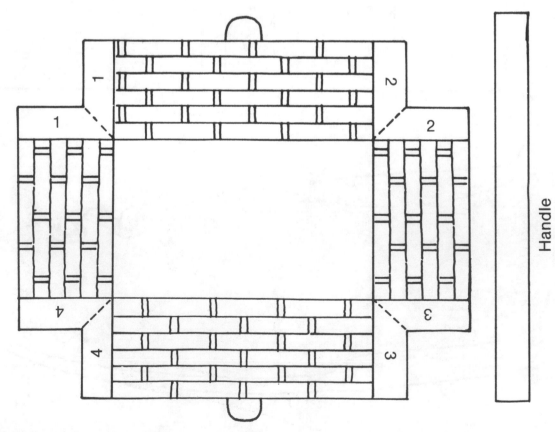

SS1818

POSSIBLE VERSE:

"...man shall not live by bread alone, but by every word of God."

Luke 4:4

"I am the living bread which came down from heaven: if any man eat of this bread, he shall live for ever: ..."

John 6:51

"And when he had taken the five loaves and the two fishes, he looked up to heaven, and blessed, and brake the loaves, ..."

Mark 6:41

SS1818

LEARNING VERSES BY "HEART"

Print a verse over and over again along the outline of this picture. Soon you will know a memory verse by heart!

MATERIALS:

Heart pattern
Tracing paper
Colored pencils or fine point markers
Four paper clips

DIRECTIONS:

1. Put a sheet of tracing paper on top of this heart picture (or any other).
2. Paper clip it in place on all four sides so that it won't move.
3. Use colored pencils or fine point markers to print a verse over and over again along the outline of the picture beneath. Use different colors on different parts of the picture.
4. Remove the paper clips and separate your picture from the pattern.
5. Write the scripture reference at the bottom of your picture.

POSSIBLE VERSES:

"...let the peace of God rule in your hearts, ..."   Colossians 3:15

"...Thou shalt love the Lord thy God with all thy heart, ..."   Matthew 22:37

"...Today if ye will hear his voice, Harden not your heart, ..."   Psalm 95:7-8

"...My heart rejoiceth in the Lord, ..."   I Samuel 2:1

Shining Star Publications, Copyright © 1990, A division of Good Apple, Inc.   SS1818

BOOKMARKS FOR SUMMER READING

Use these bookmarks for summer Bible reading and for helping you to memorize verses.

MATERIALS:

Bookmark patterns reproduced on heavy paper
Crayons or markers
Scissors
Clear Con-Tact paper or laminating materials (optional)

DIRECTIONS:

1. Write a verse on each bookmark.
2. Color and cut out each bookmark.
3. Cover with Con-Tact paper or laminating materials and cut out again. (This will keep the colors from transferring onto your book pages.) (optional)

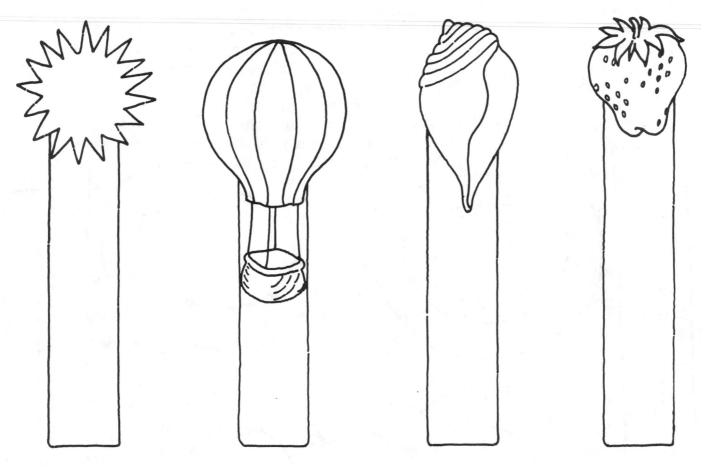

POSSIBLE VERSES:

(Sun)   ". . .let them that love him be as the sun when he goeth forth in his might. . . ."
Judges 5:31

(Balloon)   "Humble yourselves in the sight of the Lord, and he shall lift you up."
James 4:10

(Seashell)   "The Lord on high is mightier than the noise of many waters, yea, than the mighty waves of the sea."
Psalm 93:4

(Fruit)   ". . .I have chosen you, and ordained you, that ye should go and bring forth fruit, . . ."
John 15:16

SS1818

CRAFTS
SUNGLASSES FOR NOAH'S ANIMALS

Perhaps the animals on Noah's Ark could have used a pair of sunglasses when they saw sunlight for the first time after being in a dark ark for so long. Why not make several pairs for some stuffed animals? Put them on the animals and invite children from the younger classes to a "wild" animal showing. Better yet, ask young children to bring in their favorite stuffed animals. Then have the older children make sunglasses for the stuffed animals.

MATERIALS:

Patterns for sunglasses
Tagboard
Crayons or markers
Scissors
Glue
Odds and ends (glitter, sequins, scrap paper)
Colored cellophane

DIRECTIONS:

1. Cut out the patterns and trace them onto tagboard. Feel free to vary the designs a little.
2. Color and cut out the sunglasses and the arms for the sunglasses.
3. Write memory verses on the arms of the sunglasses, if desired.
4. Glue glitter, or small paper shapes (such as sea shells, beach balls, palm trees, etc.) to the sunglasses.
5. Fold back the arms at the points indicated by the dotted lines on the original patterns.
6. Glue a folded arm to each side of the front frames.
7. Glue colored cellophane to the back of the glasses to serve as lenses. (optional)

POSSIBLE VERSES:

". . .now we see through a glass, darkly; but then face to face: . . ." I Corinthians 13:12

"Let your light so shine before men, that they may see your good works, and glorify your Father which is in heaven."
Matthew 5:16

SS1818

SHIP SHAPE SUMMER

Just for fun, try reading the title of this page quickly three times in a row. Then make this summer picture.

MATERIALS:

Boat pattern
Crayons
Scissors
Glue
Construction paper scraps of various colors
A sheet of light blue construction paper (optional)

DIRECTIONS:

1. Cut triangles of various sizes from construction paper or wrapping paper scraps.
2. Glue them to the boat, sails, and flag. Leave a little space between each triangle.
3. Color the background or cut out the boat, water, and cloud and glue to a sheet of blue paper.
4. Memorize the verse.

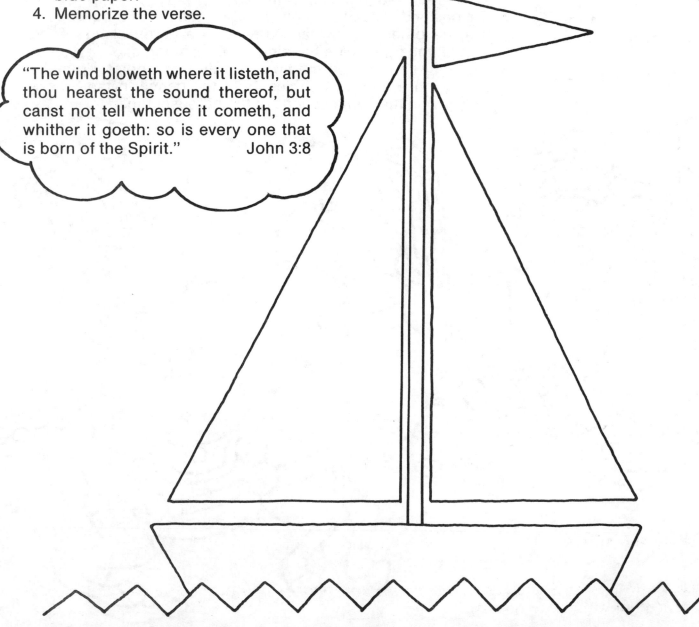

"The wind bloweth where it listeth, and thou hearest the sound thereof, but canst not tell whence it cometh, and whither it goeth: so is every one that is born of the Spirit."   John 3:8

SS1818

SUMMER CAROUSEL

This simple version of a carousel will prove to be a source of amusement when a trip to an amusement park is not possible. As a service project, your class can make extra carousels for a children's hospital, a day care center, or the younger Vacation Bible School students. Reproduce the carousel and carousel figures on tagboard or heavy white construction paper, if possible.

MATERIALS:

Carousel pattern
Patterns for three
   carousel figures
Crayons or markers
Tape
Pencil
Scissors
Thread

DIRECTIONS:

1. Color the carousel top and the three objects you'll be hanging from the carousel. You may want to make your own biblical shapes (ark animals, rainbows, etc.) or summer shapes (bicycles, fruit, etc.) instead of the ones given.
2. Cut out the carousel top and cut or punch out the tiny holes.
3. Cut along the dotted lines and bend the sections slightly upward.
4. Overlap the end sections and tape in place.
5. Cut out the three figures and cut or punch out the tiny holes.
6. Cut three 6" long pieces of thread.
7. Tie one end of each thread to a hole in the top of the carousel. Tie the other end of each thread to a carousel figure, so that all the figures are hanging at equal heights.
8. Put your carousel on the tip of a dull pencil point. To make the carousel move in circles, hold the pencil in the breeze or blow on the bent sections of the carousel top.

SS1818

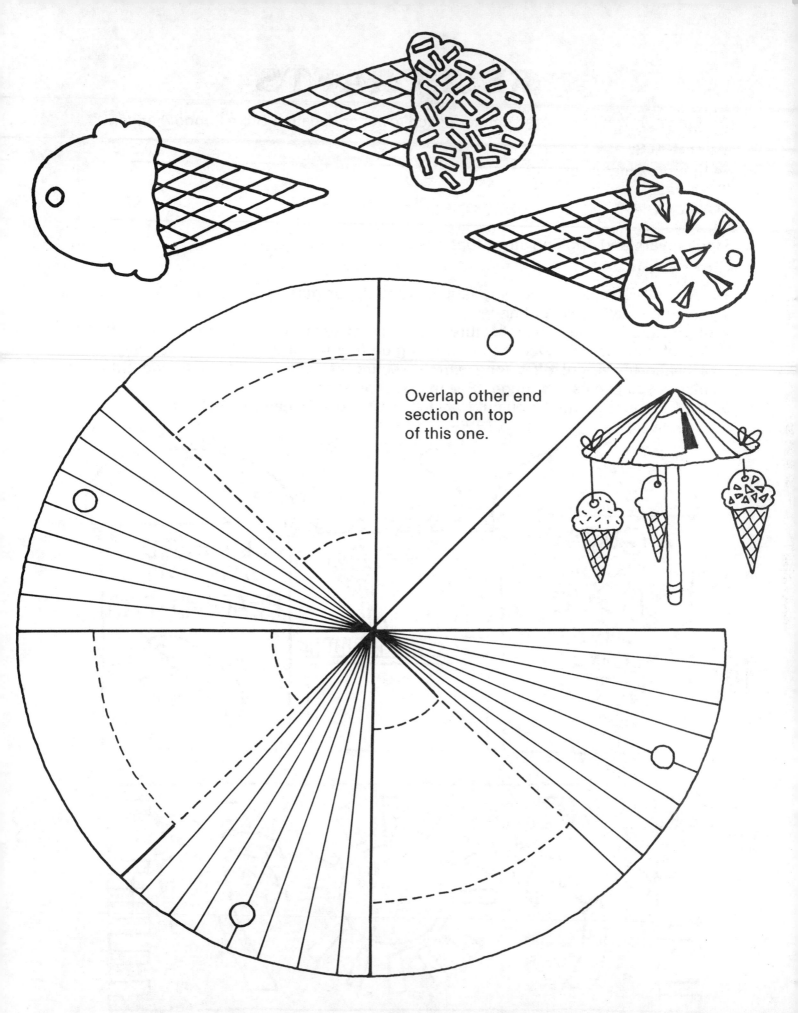

Overlap other end
section on top
of this one.

27

SS1818

FELT CRAFTS

Design your own miniature summer beach towel or Vacation Bible School banner.

MATERIALS:

Felt (approximately 9" x 12")
Felt scraps
Scissors
Glue
Stapler, yarn and drinking straw (optional)

DIRECTIONS:

1. From felt scraps, cut out any letters, symbols, or other shapes you will want to use on your beach towel or banner.
2. If you are making a banner, thread a piece of yarn through a straw. Then fold the top of your banner over the straw and glue (or staple) into place. If you are making a beach towel, cut off a long narrow section of your felt rectangle and cut it into pieces you can use as fringe. (See the illustrations.)
3. Glue the pieces which you cut from felt scraps to your banner or towel.

PUT ON A HAPPY FACE

Tell some ways "clowning around" this summer can cause injuries or hurt feelings. Share ways to put a smile on someone's face this summer. Then make this cheerful clown.

MATERIALS:

Clown pattern
Construction paper
Crayons or markers
Scissors
Glue
Odds and ends, such as yarn, bric-a-brac, sequins, paper punch dots

DIRECTIONS:

1. Color and cut out the clown.
2. Glue it to a piece of construction paper. If you want to use this as a card to give to someone who needs cheering, fold a piece of construction paper in half, and then glue the clown to the front of it.
3. Glue yarn and other odds and ends to some parts of the clown.
4. Write an appropriate message or verse on the construction paper.

POSSIBLE VERSES AND MESSAGES:

"A merry heart maketh a cheerful countenance: . . ."   Proverbs 15:13

"A merry heart doeth good like a medicine: . . ."   Proverbs 17:22

Have a happy day!

Smile, God loves you.

POSITIVE AND NEGATIVE CREATION DESIGNS

Have children make this project after studying about creation. Contrasting colors make this design appealing.

MATERIALS:

One pattern
Sheet of standard size construction paper
½ sheet construction paper of a contrasting color
Pencil
Scissors
Glue

DIRECTIONS:

1. Cut the half sheet of construction paper into four equal parts as shown.
2. Fold each piece in half lengthwise as shown.
3. Choose one of the given patterns, cut it out, and trace it onto each of the four pieces. Trace with the arrow along the fold.
4. Keep each piece folded and cut along the lines you traced. You will get a cut out section and a section with a hole from each of the four original pieces.
5. Cut all eight of your pieces along the fold.
6. Arrange the pieces on the whole sheet of paper, alternating positive and negative design as shown.
7. Glue each piece into place.
8. Write an appropriate verse on your picture. (optional)

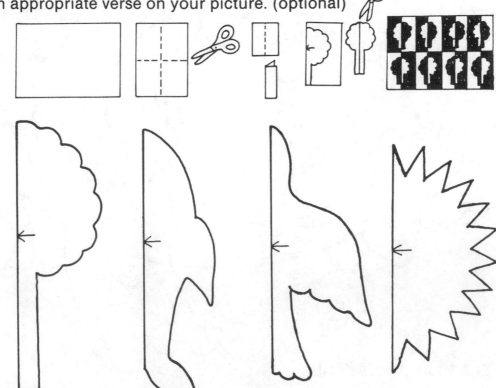

POSSIBLE VERSES:

"For by him were all things created, that are in heaven, and that are in earth, . . ."

Colossians 1:16

"And God saw every thing that he had made, and, behold, it was very good. . . ."

Genesis 1:31

SS1818

CALLED BY NAME

This activity is good for the first day of class. You will learn the names of children in your class as you watch them write their names over and over again on this art project.

MATERIALS:

Balloon pattern
Tracing paper
Four paper clips
Colored pencils or fine point markers

DIRECTIONS:

1. Put a sheet of tracing paper on top of this picture (or any other).
2. Clip it in place on all four sides so that it won't move.
3. Use colored pencils or fine point markers to print your name over and over again along the outline of the picture. Use different colors on different parts of the picture.
4. Remove the paper clips and separate your picture from the pattern.
5. Write an appropriate verse at the bottom of your picture.

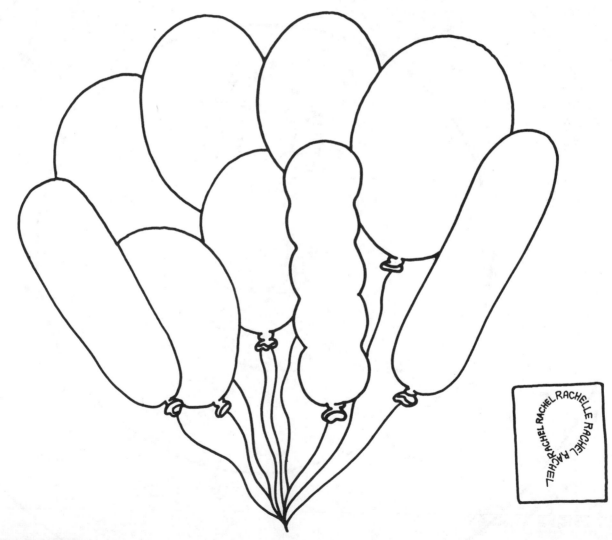

POSSIBLE VERSE:

". . .Fear not: for I have redeemed thee, I have called thee by thy name; thou art mine."

Isaiah 43:1

SS1818

DAISY WREATH

You can hang this wreath on a door or set it in the middle of a table as part of a centerpiece. You may want to put a candle or small bowl in the middle if you use it as a table decoration.

MATERIALS:

Ring pattern and daisy patterns reproduced on heavy paper
Crayons or markers
Scissors
Glue

DIRECTIONS:

1. Color and cut out the wreath and the daisies.
2. Glue the daisies to the wreath.

 SS1818

DAISY NAPKIN RINGS

You may want to use these napkin rings with your daisy wreath/centerpiece.

MATERIALS:

Daisy patterns
Paper tube
Scissors
Crayons or markers
Glue
Paper (Con-Tact paper, construction paper, or wrapping paper)

DIRECTIONS:

1. Cut a paper tube into 1" wide sections as shown.
2. Glue paper around each ring.
3. Color and cut out the daisies.
4. Glue one to each ring.

Shining Star Publications, Copyright © 1990, A division of Good Apple, Inc.

SS1818

SPORTING GOODS

These patterns have a number of uses. Reproduce on heavy paper. Then use them in some of the following ways.

MATERIALS:

Equipment patterns
Hole punch
Yarn
Paper
Crayons or markers

DIRECTIONS:

1. Punch holes in the patterns and tie yarn to them. Children on the same team can wear the same pattern to help them identify teammates.
2. Write ways to be a good sport on each piece of equipment. Some examples: *I can be cheerful when I lose. I can choose someone first to be on my team, even though he/she is usually one of the last to be chosen.*
3. Words to a verse can be written a few words at a time on the pieces before they are reproduced. Children can put the verse in order. The pieces can be numbered on the back, so that the activity can be self-checking.

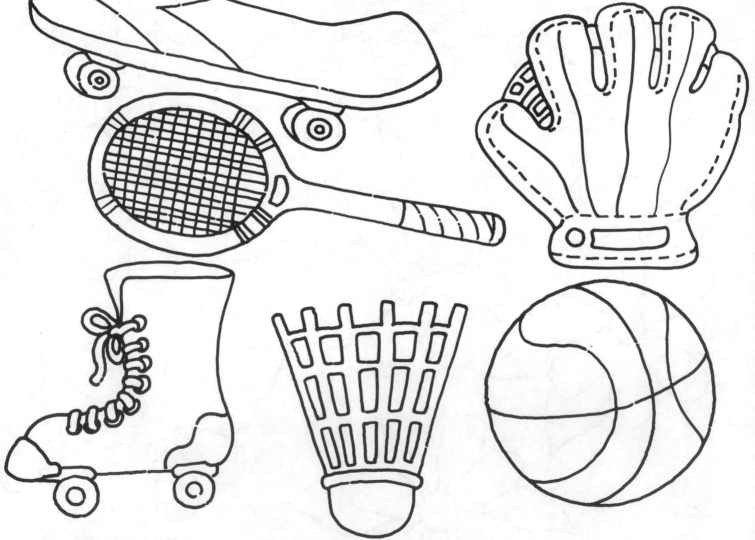

POSSIBLE VERSES:

". . .whatsoever ye do, do all to the glory of God."   I Corinthians 10:31

"Make a joyful noise unto the Lord, all the earth: make a loud noise, and rejoice, and sing praise."   Psalm 98:4

SS1818

SING OF SUMMER

Hold this picture up to the sun or place it in a sunny window. It will "sing" out with color.

MATERIALS:

Music patterns
Black construction paper
Tape
Colored tissue paper
Scissors
Pencil
White crayon or China marker (optional)

DIRECTIONS:

1. Cut out the patterns.
2. Arrange the pieces as shown on a piece of black construction paper. The letters should be arranged to spell *SING*!
3. Trace all the pieces onto the black paper and then cut them out.
4. Tape pieces of colored tissue paper behind the cut out sections.
5. Use a white crayon or China marker to write a verse at the bottom. (optional)

POSSIBLE VERSES:

"O sing unto the Lord a new song: sing unto the Lord, all the earth." Psalm 96:1

"Serve the Lord with gladness: come before his presence with singing." Psalm 100:2

SS1818

SUMMER AND BIBLICAL DESIGNS

Make a design of an object from a Bible story you've studied recently or a summer object you like.

MATERIALS:

Pattern
Crayons or markers
Scissors
White paper

DIRECTIONS:

1. Use a crayon or marker to draw the outline of a summer or biblical object in the middle of a white sheet of paper. (If you want, you can cut and trace one of the objects below to get you started.)
2. Use different colors to repeat the outline around the original one.
3. Continue enlarging the design all the way to the edge of the paper.

SS1818

POPSICLE CARD POP-UP

Give or send this Popsicle pop-up to a friend.

MATERIALS:

Popsicle pattern
Boy or girl pattern
Crayons or markers
Scissors
Glue

DIRECTIONS:

1. Color and cut out the Popsicle and the boy or girl.
2. Fold the boy or girl back on the dotted lines.
3. Fold the Popsicle forward along the dotted lines.
4. Glue the boy or girl tabs to the Popsicle circles.
5. On the Popsicle stick on the right, write "From: _____."
6. Close the card and write "To: _____" on the Popsicle stick in front.

Keep "Cool" This Summer!

SS1818

LET THE SUN SHINE IN

The sun will shine through the tiny pinholes in this summer picture.

MATERIALS:

Pattern
Straight pin
Four paper clips
Scissors
Dark sheet of construction paper

DIRECTIONS:

1. Cut out the picture below and place it on top of a dark sheet of construction paper.
2. Clip the two papers together on all sides.
3. Use a pin to punch holes through both layers at every point indicated on the pattern.
4. Remove the paper clips and the pattern.
5. Hold your construction paper up outside on a sunny day or hang it in a window that gets lots of sunlight.

Shining Star Publications, Copyright © 1990, A division of Good Apple, Inc.   SS1818

BEACH BALL DAZZLERS

The designs on these beach balls will do interesting things as they twirl around.

MATERIALS:

Patterns (reproduced
  on tagboard or white
  construction paper)
Markers
Scissors
Pencil

DIRECTIONS:

1. Use brightly colored markers to color the beach balls.
2. Cut out the beach balls.
3. Use a pencil to poke a small hole in the center of each one.
4. Balance one of the beach balls on the pencil point and hold the pencil between the palms of your hands.
5. Rub your palms back and forth against each other so that the pencil rotates. The designs on the beach ball should make interesting patterns as they twirl around.

Shining Star Publications, Copyright © 1990, A division of Good Apple, Inc.

SS1818

THE GARDEN OF HIS LOVE

Reproduce these stencils on tagboard or heavy construction paper, if possible. Use the stencils for the project below or use them to decorate stationery, storage containers, wrapping paper, etc.

MATERIALS:

Flower patterns
Scissors
Colored tissue paper
Tape
Black construction paper
Four paper clips
Colored pencil

DIRECTIONS:

1. Carefully cut out each tiny flower piece and discard. Be careful not to cut through the rest of the paper. It will serve as a stencil.
2. After you have cut out the small pieces, clip this stencil page, on all four sides, to the top of a black sheet of construction paper.
3. Use a pencil to trace each stencil onto the black construction paper.
4. Remove the paper clips and the stencil patterns.
5. Carefully cut out the tiny pieces you drew on the black construction paper and discard them.
6. Tape tissue paper of various colors behind the holes.
7. If you want to, write a verse on the construction paper.
8. Hang your project in a window and let the sun shine through.

POSSIBLE VERSE:

". . .even Solomon in all his glory was not arrayed like one of these." Matthew 6:29

FINGERPRINT PICTURES

Your fingerprints are unique. So are your talents and abilities. Use your fingerprints to create a unique biblical or summer scene.

MATERIALS:

White paper
Washable ink
Ink pad
Pencils
Crayons or markers

DIRECTIONS:

1. Use pencils, pens, or markers to sketch a picture. Be sure to leave areas where fingerprints can be incorporated into your sketch.
2. Pour washable or non-waterproof ink on an empty ink pad.
3. Put your finger(s) on the ink pad and then press onto your picture.
4. Write a verse at the bottom, if appropriate.

POSSIBLE VERSES:

". . .every man hath his proper gift of God, . . ."   I Corinthians 7:7

"There went in two and two unto Noah into the ark, . . ."   Genesis 7:9

SUNSHINE PICTURES

Talk about the joy of summer and sunshine. Then let children complete this craft.

MATERIALS:

Sunshine picture pattern (reproduced on tagboard or white construction paper, if possible)
Markers or crayons
Colored tissue paper
Scissors
Glue

DIRECTIONS:

1. Color the picture with markers or crayons.
2. Loosely roll 1" squares of colored tissue paper into balls.
3. Spread glue onto a small area of the picture and cover it with the tissue paper balls.
4. Repeat, using different colors for different parts of the picture. Leave some parts uncovered and let the crayon or marker colors show on those parts.
5. Glue tissue paper balls to the tiny circles between the verse words.

NOAH'S BALLOON ZOO

Give each child a balloon or two to blow up. Have various shapes available. Provide tape and scraps of paper, yarn, etc., with which to decorate the balloons as animals. For practice, children may want to sketch some animals on the balloons below.

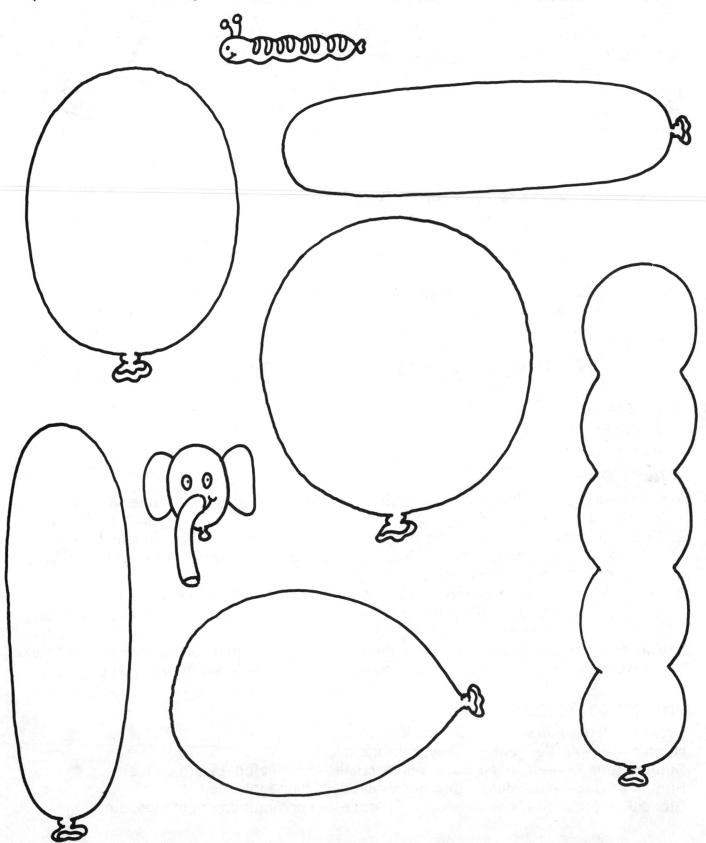

SS1818

CRAFT DOUGH RECIPE

You can use this dough immediately or make it a day or two ahead of time and store in a plastic bag or covered bowl until it is ready for use.

MATERIALS:

(Per child)
½ cup flour
¼ cup salt
⅙ cup water
Measuring cup
Mixing utensil
Bowl for mixing ingredients
Food coloring (optional)

DIRECTIONS:

1. Decide whether to let each child make his or her own craft dough or adjust the recipe and make enough dough, yourself, for your entire class.
2. Mix the salt and flour together in a bowl.
3. Add water to the mixture, a little at a time. If you want colored dough, first add food coloring to the water.
4. Knead the craft dough with your hands. Add a little more flour if it is too sticky or a little more water if it is too dry.

CRAFT DOUGH CREATIONS

MATERIALS:

Craft dough
Aluminum foil

DIRECTIONS:

1. Work on top of a piece of aluminum foil. Mold craft dough into one or more of the objects suggested on the next page.
2. Allow the projects to dry for a few days or bake them on a cookie sheet in an oven set at 225⁰ for about an hour. (Time will vary according to the number and thickness of the objects you are baking.)
3. Leave plain or color with markers or poster paints and allow to dry.
4. You can cover your project with a few coats of clear nail polish to make it last longer and to keep the color from coming off.
5. Add any magnets, safety pins, yarn, markers, tape, paint, nail polish, pencils, toothpicks, cookie sheet, etc. needed on your project. (See sample ideas on the next page.)

POSSIBLE THEMES:

Creation—star, moon, sun, flowers, fish, birds, etc.
Noah's Ark—giraffe, goat, donkey, zebra, etc.
Summertime fun—baseball, sailboat, seashells, watermelon, beach ball, etc.
Summer fruits—watermelon, orange, strawberry, pineapple, etc.
Biblical objects—rainbow, sheep, heart, dove, ten commandment stones, etc.

Shining Star Publications, Copyright © 1990, A division of Good Apple, Inc.

SS1818

CRAFT DOUGH PROJECTS

MINIATURE VERSION
Simply make the object in miniature form.

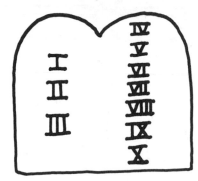

PENCIL TOP
Make a small version of something. Poke a hole halfway through it with a pencil. Slip the project over a pencil after it has been dried and colored.

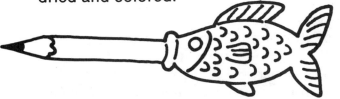

(Use the curved end of the bobby pin to make scales.)

BUTTONS AND PINS
Make a flat version of the object or draw it on a flat circle. Use a toothpick to cut a picture or message into the circle. Use strong tape to attach a safety pin to the back of the object after it has been dried and colored.

FRONT   BACK

MAGNETS
Add a piece of magnetic tape to the back of the object after it has been dried and colored.

FRONT   BACK

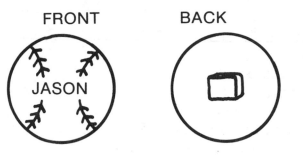

NECKLACES AND MEDALLIONS
Poke a hole near the top with a pencil or straw. Add string or yarn after the object has been dried and colored.

MOBILE
Make objects relating to a specific theme. Use a pencil or straw to poke a hole near the top of each one. Tie yarn or string to each after drying and coloring. Hang from a hanger or something else.

Shining Star Publications, Copyright © 1990, A division of Good Apple, Inc.   SS1818

SAND PAINTING

For this summertime project, children can use the biblical scene below, or they may want to draw their own beach scene or desert scene to cover with colored sand (or salt).

MATERIALS:

Pattern
Thin cardboard
Glue
Crayons or markers
Scissors
Plastic spoons
Bucket of water for rinsing hands
Paper towels for cleanup
Containers of colored sand or colored salt

DIRECTIONS:

1. Color and cut out the scene below and glue it to thin cardboard. (You can draw your own scene on the cardboard if you want.)
2. Spread paper towels in the area where you'll be working.
3. Spread glue evenly and thinly over the part of the picture you want to color with the first color of sand or salt.
4. Spoon some of the sand or salt onto the glue.
5. Bend the picture slightly and pour the loose sand or salt back into the container.
6. Use other colors to cover some of the other sections of your picture in the same manner.

DESERT SAND CRAFT JAR

This is a simple summer project your children will enjoy making outside on a picnic table.

MATERIALS:

Sand of various colors
Containers filled with salt which have been colored with food coloring and allowed to dry
A small clear jar or goldfish bowl
Plastic spoons
Pencil
Odds and ends to decorate the lid (optional)

DIRECTIONS:

1. Spoon a little of one color sand or salt into the bottom of a dry bowl or jar.
2. Spoon other colors into the jar, one layer at a time.
3. Mound the sand or salt in some areas to form pretty patterns. In some places, make it drop into the previous layer by using a pencil point to push down the sand near the glass.
4. Fill the container as high as you want, but do not shake it. Set it where it is unlikely to get bumped.
5. Cover the lid with felt, bric-a-brac, artifical flowers, or any odds and ends desired. (optional)

SUMMER KEEPSAKE CONTAINER

Use this container to store summer items found on trips, hikes, etc., or give it to someone as a gift.

MATERIALS:

Round ice cream container and lid
Glue
Scissors
Construction paper
Small seashells or spray painted macaroni shells
A paper fastener and a large bead (optional)

DIRECTIONS:

1. Cover the lid of a round container with construction paper. (You can use the lid to trace a circle onto the construction paper.) You will also need a strip of construction paper to cover the edge of the lid.
2. An optional handle can be added to the lid. Insert a paper fastener through a large bead. Punch a small hole in the middle of the lid and insert the paper fastener. Spread the arms of the paper fastener once it is inserted.
3. Cut the ice cream container to the height desired.
4. Cut a piece of construction paper to fit the remaining portion of the container and glue it on.
5. Glue seashells or macaroni to the container and its lid.

Shining Star Publications, Copyright © 1990, A division of Good Apple, Inc. SS1818

SEASHELL PICTURE FRAME

Use this frame for a favorite verse, picture, or photo.

MATERIALS:

Pattern
Small seashells or
 spray painted mac-
 aroni shells
Scissors
Glue
Crayons or markers
Poster board
White paper

DIRECTIONS:

1. Cut out the picture frame pattern and trace it onto the poster board.
2. Cut out the poster board frame you have traced.
3. Put some glue on the back of the frame and paste a white sheet of paper to it.
4. Trim off any excess white paper which may be sticking out behind the frame.
5. In your fanciest printing, write a verse on the white paper.
6. Glue sea shells or macaroni shells in a pretty pattern around the frame.

POSSIBLE VERSE:

"Many, O Lord my God, are thy wonderful works. . . ."   Psalm 40:5

SS1818

FISH DESIGNS

Create interesting and uniquely painted fish. This is a great project to go along with the story of creation or lessons on individuality.

MATERIALS:

Patterns
Blue construction paper
Scissors
Glue
Watercolor paints or thin tempera paints
Newspaper or wax paper to cover the area for working

DIRECTIONS:

1. Cut out the fish patterns.
2. Fold each fish back along the dotted line and set on top of paper to keep the area where you are working clean.
3. Sprinkle a few drops of watercolor paints or thin tempera paints on one half of each fish. Make sure you put the paint on the blank side, not the side with the dotted lines.
4. Refold along the crease and rub your fingers back and forth along each closed fish.
5. Open the fish to see the pretty patterns.
6. Let the paint dry and then glue each fish to a sheet of blue construction paper.

SS1818

REPEATED SUMMER AND BIBLICAL PATTERNS

Use a summer pattern or a pattern that goes along with the Bible stories you are studying. For example, the fish could be used if you are studying about creation, the multiplication of the loaves and fish, the great catch of fish, etc.

MATERIALS:

One pattern
Thin cardboard
Scissors
Crayons or markers
White paper

DIRECTIONS:

1. Cut out one of the patterns.
2. Trace it onto a piece of cardboard.
3. Cut out the cardboard shape.
4. Put the cardboard shape onto the white paper and use a crayon or marker to trace around the shape. You can trace neatly around the edges or use a jagged type of tracing procedure as shown.
5. Move the cardboard pattern and repeat with different colors. Overlap the patterns.

POSSIBLE VERSES:

". . .I will multiply thy seed as the stars of the heaven, . . ." Genesis 22:17

". . .Follow me, and I will make you fishers of men." Matthew 4:19

THE WORK OF YOUR HAND

You may want to incorporate the given verse, or part of it, into your pottery design.

MATERIALS:
Pottery pattern
Scissors
Markers, paints, crayons, or chalk

DIRECTIONS:
1. Sketch a design onto the pottery.
2. Color with crayons, markers, paint, or chalk.
3. Cut out the pottery.

POSSIBLE VERSE:
"But now, O Lord, thou art our father; we are the clay, and thou our potter; and we all are the work of thy hand."
Isaiah 64:8

OPTIONAL:
Make a small bowl out of craft dough. The directions for making craft dough can be found on page 44. Use a toothpick to make designs or to write the given verse on your bowl. After your bowl has been baked or dried, use it to store small items. For a service project, you may even try to grow a plant in your bowl to take to someone at a nursing home. Be sure to put a small plastic pot inside the bowl.

 SS1818

SUMMER FAN/LANTERN

Use this pattern to make a fan for cooling off on a hot, summer day, or use it to make a paper lantern.

MATERIALS:

Pattern
Crayons
Scissors
Writing utensil for
    writing verse words
Stapler
For lantern:
    crepe paper or tis-
    sue paper
    strip of construction
    paper about 12"
    long and 1" wide

DIRECTIONS:

1. Write a memory verse along the top of the fan.
2. Color and cut out the pattern.
3. Option 1—To make a fan, fold along the dotted lines accordian style and staple at the bottom.
   Option 2—To make a lantern, fold the pattern in half as shown. Cut along the dotted lines. Unfold and form into a type of cylinder. Staple the end slits together. Staple the narrow strip to the top of the lantern to form a handle. Cut and staple strips of crepe paper or tissue paper to the bottom.

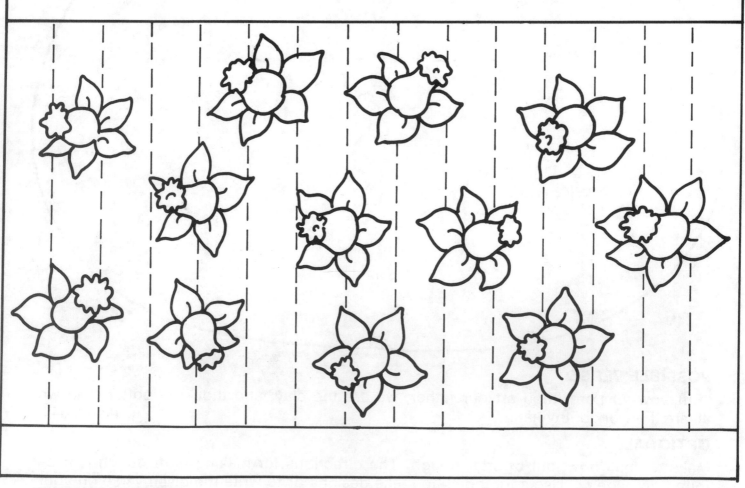

POSSIBLE VERSE:

"This is the day which the Lord hath made; we will rejoice and be glad in it."

Psalm 118:24

SS1818

PAPER PUNCH PICTURES

The colorful dots on this project will brighten a room like sunshine.

MATERIALS:

Pencil
Paper punch
Brightly colored paper
    scraps
Black sheet of con-
    struction paper
Glue
White   sharpened
    crayon or China
    marker (optional)

DIRECTIONS:

1. Use a regular pencil (so the lines don't show later) to draw a simple picture of a summer or biblical object on the black paper.
2. Use a paper punch to punch out small dots of various colors from the scraps of paper.
3. Put tiny dots of glue (about 15 at a time) along the outline of your drawing. Leave a tiny space between each dot.
4. Put a paper punch dot on each dot of glue. Repeat until the dots form the entire outline of your picture. You can fill in some sections with dots, if appropriate.
5. Use a white crayon or China marker to write a verse that goes along with your picture. (optional)

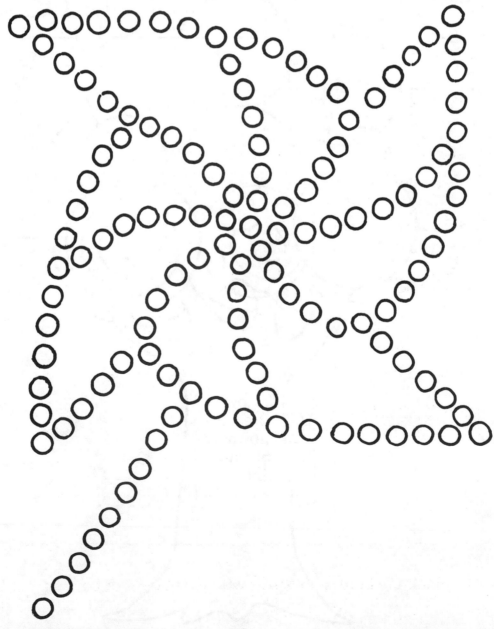

Shining Star Publications, Copyright © 1990, A division of Good Apple, Inc.

SS1818

SUMMER TREE

Celebrate your own individuality. Make each part of this tree special and unique.

MATERIALS:

Tree pattern
Crayons or markers
Scissors
Glue
Construction paper

DIRECTIONS:

1. Use crayons or markers to decorate each circle differently. Make a variety of designs and summer objects (softballs, marbles, soccer balls, dart boards, oranges, etc.)
2. Cut out the tree and glue it to a piece of construction paper.
3. Memorize the verse.

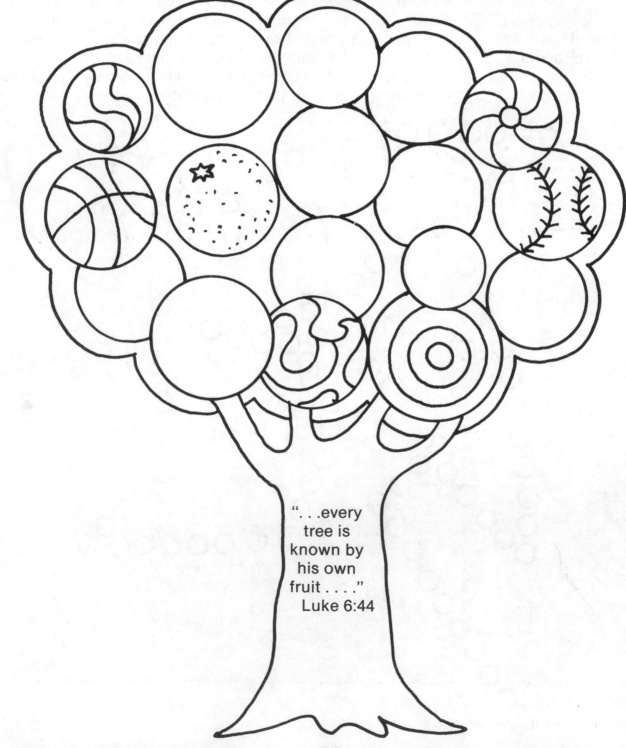

". . .every tree is known by his own fruit . . . ."
Luke 6:44

SS1818

SUNFLOWER SEED PICTURE

Study Bible stories about seeds (The Mustard Seed, The Sower, etc.) Then bring out the seeds and let your children complete this project.

MATERIALS:

Sunflower picture
Scissors
Cardboard
Glue
Seeds and/or small natural objects such as rice

DIRECTIONS:

1. Cut out the picture and glue it to a piece of cardboard.
2. Glue a variety of small seeds to the picture.
3. Write an appropriate verse at the bottom of your picture.

POSSIBLE VERSE:

"The sower soweth the word."

Mark 4:14

SS1818

SUNSET SCENES

MATERIALS:

Watercolors
Paintbrush
White paper
Black construction paper
Pencil (a color that will show up on black)
Scissors
Glue

DIRECTIONS:

1. Paint streaks of sunset colors across a white sheet of paper and then set the paper aside to dry.
2. Cut out the desert scene below and trace it onto black construction paper. (You may want to draw your own desert scene, palm tree scene, or sailboat scene instead.)
3. Cut the scene from the black construction paper.
4. Glue the scene to your dry painting.
5. Cut out the verse and glue it to your picture.

"From the rising of the sun unto the going down of the same the Lord's name is to be praised."

Psalm 113:3

SS1818

SUMMER VACATION BIBLE TRIP

Take an imaginary trip to the Holy Land. Read about various places in your Bible. Then design a bumper sticker, postcard, road sign, window sticker, souvenir pennant, and T-shirt to go along with the places you have "visited." A sample idea has been given for each item, but try to think of your own. Take your creations home in the paper suitcase. Some options are to display some of them on a class bulletin board or use the pieces to form a mobile. Reproduce on heavy construction paper, if possible.

MATERIALS:

Bible
Vacation patterns
Pencil
Crayons or markers
Scissors
Glue

DIRECTIONS:

1. Read several Bible stories and make special note of the locations where the stories take place.
2. Draw "stickers" on your suitcase of some of the places you "visited." Color the suitcase.
3. Cut out the suitcase and fold back along the dotted lines.
4. Put glue on the suitcase tabs, and glue the tabs, which are numbered the same, together.
5. Make designs and/or write sayings on the remaining pieces.
6. Cut them out and store in the suitcase.

```
         2                    2


   ". . .Go ye into all the world, and
   preach the gospel to every crea-
   ture."

   Mark 16:15



Mark 16:15



         1                    1
```

POSTCARD FRONT (PICTURE), BACK (MESSAGE)

Sample: Greetings from Siloam! Today, a man named Jesus told me to visit the pool of Siloam. There I was cured of my blindness, so now I'm taking in the "sights." Can't wait to "see" you! (See John 9:1-11)

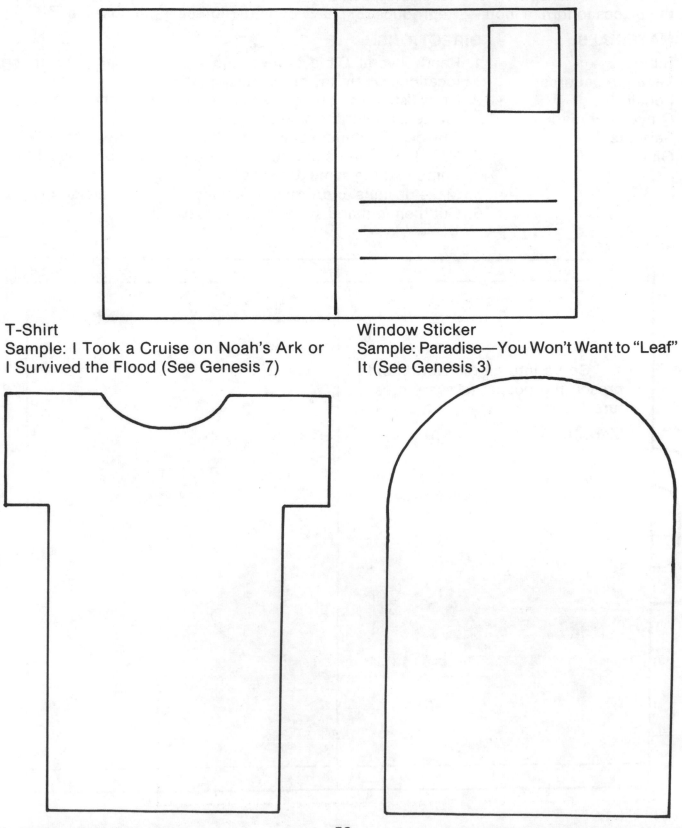

T-Shirt
Sample: I Took a Cruise on Noah's Ark or I Survived the Flood (See Genesis 7)

Window Sticker
Sample: Paradise—You Won't Want to "Leaf" It (See Genesis 3)

SS1818

PENNANT

Sample: Souvenir of the "World" Series Day 5 (See Genesis 1:20-23)

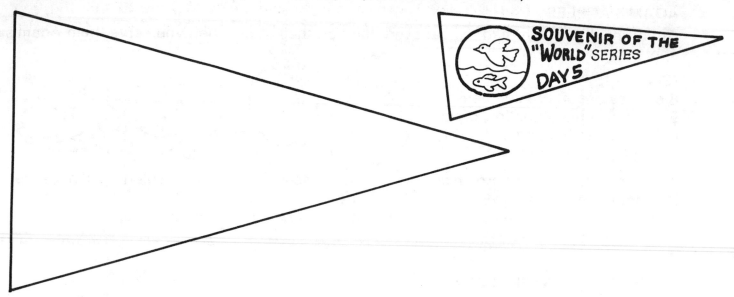

ROAD SIGN

Sample: Leaving Sodom City Limits—There's No Turning Back! (See Genesis 19:17-26)

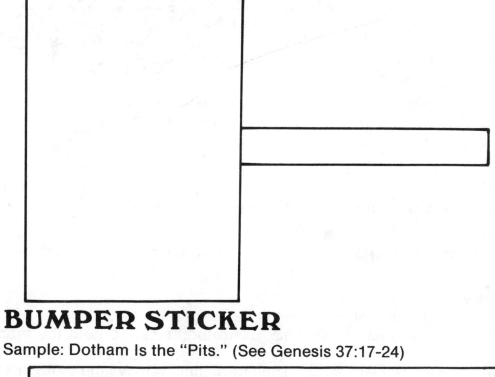

BUMPER STICKER

Sample: Dotham Is the "Pits." (See Genesis 37:17-24)

SNACKS

ADAM'S APPLES

Children will be "tempted" to eat everything on their plate when you serve them Adam's apples.

(Serves 15)
8 ounces of soft cream cheese
9 ounces of marshmallow cream
6 Granny Smith apples
6 Red Delicious apples

1. Thoroughly mix soft cream cheese and marshmallow cream (with a blender, if possible).
2. Spoon mixture onto 15 small paper plates.
3. Slice apples into 8-12 sections each and put a few slices on each plate.
4. Dip the apples and eat.

GARDEN OF "EATEN" SALAD

Children won't want to stop until all of this salad is "eaten."

(Serves 15)
4 cups plain yogurt
4 tablespoons mayonnaise
4 teaspoons honey
8 grated carrots
4 large apples, cubed
1 cup raisins
1 cup chopped walnuts

1. In a large bowl, mix yogurt, mayonnaise, and honey until well-blended.
2. Add carrots, apples, raisins, and walnuts. Stir until everything is well-coated.
3. Spoon onto 15 small plates and enjoy!

NOAH'S ANIMAL "PEARS"

Give children a pair of pears and let them create some delicious snacks.

2 canned pear halves per child
Food decorations such as raisins, curled carrot strips, nuts, cherries, marshmallows, etc.

1. Give each child a plate with two pear halves.
2. Set bowls of food decorations and toothpicks in the center of the table.
3. Let children decorate their pears as ark animals, using toothpicks to hold the food garnishes in place.
4. Let children admire everyone's animal "pears." Then have them remove the toothpicks and eat.

SS1818

PETER'S PEANUT BUTTER "FLOAT"

Children will want to "sink" right into this dessert drink.

(Serves 15)
3 cups creamy peanut butter
6 cups cold milk
6 ripe bananas
3 pints softened vanilla ice cream
15 maraschino cherries

1. In a large bowl, beat peanut butter and milk together with an egg beater.
2. Mash bananas with a fork and add to the mixture.
3. Add softened ice cream and beat again.
4. Pour into 15 cups and float a cherry on top of each serving.

SUN/FLOWER/STAR SNACKS

Arrange fruit slices to make a sun, a flower, or a star (Whatever goes best with the Bible themes you are covering at the moment.)

(Per child)
6-8 peach or orange slices
¼ cup cottage cheese
1 tablespoon toasted sunflower seeds

1. On a small plate, arrange the fruit slices in the form of a flower, the sun's rays, or a star.
2. Put ¼ cup cottage cheese in the center.
3. Sprinkle the sunflower seeds on top of the cottage cheese.

FRUIT SALAD

Use sour cream as part of the dressing in this fruit salad or use whipped cream to give it a sweeter taste. You can add more dressing or more fruit according to preference.

(Serves 15)
1 pint whipped cream (or sour cream)
12 ounces of soft cream cheese
32 ounces of mandarin oranges
64 ounces of fruit cocktail (or fresh grapes, cherries, cubed apples, and pineapple chunks)
½ cup chopped walnuts or pecans (optional)
¼ cup coconut (optional)
1 cup of small marshmallows (optional)

1. In a large bowl, thoroughly mix together the whipped cream (or sour cream) and the soft cream cheese. Use a mixer, if possible.
2. Drain all fruit. Then add the fruit, but not the fruit juice, to the mixture.
3. Stir all the ingredients together. Separate into individual servings and eat immediately or refrigerate the whole bowl overnight and eat chilled.

SS1818

BITE-SIZED BASEBALLS

For energy, try these on a day when you play the Bible Ball Game found on page 74.

(Makes about 40 small balls)
3 cups vanilla wafer crumbs (about 70 wafers)
1 cup chopped walnuts
1½ cups powdered sugar
¼ cup unsweetened cocoa powder
6 tablespoons orange juice
3 tablespoons honey

1. Put several wafers in a plastic bag and crunch with a rolling pin. Put the crumbs in a large bowl. Repeat with all wafers.
2. Add 1 (of the 1½ cups) of powdered sugar, the ¼ cup of cocoa powder, and the chopped nuts. Stir.
3. Add the orange juice and honey and blend well.
4. Shape in small balls. (Use about 1 tablespoon of mixture to form each one.)
5. Roll balls in the remaining ½ cup of powdered sugar.

WIDOW'S MITE SNACKS

Two cucumber "coins" are used in the making of each of these snacks.

(Makes 48 hors d'oeuvres)
8 ounces of whipped cream cheese
4 dozen cracked wheat crackers (or any other kind)
4 cucumbers
Salt and pepper (optional)

1. Spread some whipped cream cheese on each cracker.
2. Cut cucumbers into slices (about the thickness of coins).
3. Put 2 cucumber "coins" or "mites" on each cracker.
4. Sprinkle salt and pepper on the cucumber slices (optional).

RAINBOW PROMISE PUNCH

This rainbow punch promises to be a crowd-pleaser.

(Makes about 35, 4-ounce servings)
64 ounces chilled fruit punch
6-ounce can of frozen lemonade
2 liters of chilled ginger ale
ice cubes
1 pint rainbow sherbert

1. In a large punch bowl or cooking pot, stir fruit punch and lemonade until the lemonade concentrate is thawed.
2. Add ginger ale and stir again.
3. Add ice cubes and scoops of sherbert.

SS1818

SONGS
IT'S THE GOOD OLD SUMMERTIME

(Sung to the tune of "Oh My Darling, Clementine")

Water gleaming, sunshine beaming,
Fluffy clouds up in the sky,
Green grass growing, breezes blowing . . .
It's the good old summertime.

Riding waves, exploring caves,
Building castles in the sand,
Catching fishes, making wishes . . .
It's the good old summertime.

Oars a-rowing, the sound of mowing,
Tasty oranges, tangy limes,
Games of ball, sunflowers tall. . .
It's the good old summertime.

MY JESUS

(Sung to the tune of "My Bonnie")

This is a good camp song. Start from a sitting position. Stand up the first time you sing a word containing *S*. Sit the next time you sing a word containing *S*. Continue standing and sitting throughout the song.

Verse:
My Jesus is there when I call Him.
My Jesus is there when I pray.
My Jesus is there when I need Him.
My Jesus is with me all day.

Refrain:
Jesus, Jesus,
Jesus is with me to stay, to stay.
Jesus, Jesus,
Jesus is with me to stay.

 SS1818

SONG OF NOAH

(Sung to the tune of "London Bridge")

God told Noah, "Build a boat.
Build a boat, Build a boat.
Make it strong so it will float,
My dear Noah."

God told Noah, "It's gonna rain,
Gonna rain, gonna rain.
Gather animals and gather grain,
My dear Noah."

God told Noah, "You won't drown,
You won't drown, You won't drown.
Get in the ark when the rain comes down,
My dear Noah."

God told Noah, "I'll shut you in,
Shut you in, shut you in.
The rest of the world will drown for their sins,
My dear Noah."

For forty days the rain came down,
Rain came down, rain came down.
Water covered every inch of ground,
My dear Noah.

Then the waters went away,
Went away, went away.
God said, "Noah, come out today,
My dear Noah."

Noah thanked the Lord on high,
Lord on high, Lord on high.
And God put a rainbow in the sky,
My dear Noah.

SS1818

HEROES TEN

(Sung to the tune of "This Old Man")

Sing the refrain after each verse.

VERSE 1:
A man named Moses
Is hero number one.
God gave him ten commandments,
For each and every one.

VERSE 2:
A man named Noah
Is hero number two.
He built an ark
That served as a zoo.

VERSE 3:
A man named Abraham
Is hero number three.
His descendants were as many as
The stars that he could see.

VERSE 4:
A man named Joshua
Is hero number four.
He made the walls of Jericho
Tumble to the floor.

VERSE 5:
A man named Jonah
Is hero number five.
He was swallowed by a whale
But came out of it alive.

VERSE 6:
A man named Gideon
Is hero number six.
For his army,
Three hundred men were picked.

VERSE 7:
A man named Jacob
Is hero number seven.
He dreamed of a ladder
That reached up to heaven.

VERSE 8:
A man named David
Is hero number eight.
With a sling and a stone
He slew a giant great.

VERSE 9:
A man named Joseph
Is hero number nine.
His father gave him
A coat so fine.

VERSE 10:
A man named Daniel
Is hero number ten.
He was thrown into
A lion's den.

REFRAIN:
He had hope and trust and faith in God above.
So this good man received God's love.

SS1818

SONG OF JESUS

(Sung to the tune of "She'll Be Comin 'Round the Mountain")

Sing any or all of the verses. Let the children make up some verses of their own.

VERSE 1:
He was laid in a manger at His birth.
He was laid in a manger at His birth.
He was laid in a manger. He was laid in a manger.
He was laid in a manger at His birth.

OTHER VERSES:
He amazed all the scholars as a lad . . .
He was baptized in the Jordan by John . . .
He was tempted in the desert three times . . .
He said to His disciples, "Follow me . . ."
He changed water into wine at a feast . . .
He spoke to the wind and calmed a storm . . .
He cured many people, sick and lame . . .
He told the little children, "Come to Me . . ."
He entered Jerusalem on a colt . . .
He told stories of the kingdom to the crowds . . .
He had his last supper with the twelve . . .
He was betrayed by Judas for some coins . . .
He was taken away and he was scourged . . .
He was nailed to the cross and there he died . . .
He rose from the dead on the third day . . .
He'll be coming once again in the end . . .

LAST VERSE:
And we'll all go out to meet Him when he
    comes.
Yes, we'll all go out to meet Him when he
    comes.
Oh, we'll all go out to meet Him. Yes, we'll
    all go out to meet Him.
Oh, we'll all go out to meet Him when he
    comes.

SS1818

THE BIBLE SONG

(Sung to the tune of "B-I-N-G-O")

There is a book that talks of faith.
The Bible is its name-o.
B-I-B-L-E, B-I-B-L-E, B-I-B-L-E,
The Bible is its name-o.

There is a book that talks of truth.
The Bible is its name-o.
(Clap)-I-B-L-E, (Clap)-I-B-L-E,(Clap)-I-B-L-E,
The Bible is its name-o.

There is a book that talks of hope.
The Bible is its name-o.
(Clap, clap)-B-L-E, (Clap, clap)-B-L-E, (Clap, clap)-B-L-E,
The Bible is its name-o.

There is a book that talks of peace.
The Bible is its name-o.
(Clap, clap, clap)-L-E, (Clap, clap, clap)-L-E, (Clap, clap, clap)-L-E,
The Bible is its name-o.

There is a book that tells of life.
The Bible is its name-o.
(Clap, clap, clap, clap)-E, (Clap, clap, clap, clap)-E, (Clap, clap, clap, clap)-E,
The Bible is its name-o.

There is a book that talks of love.
The Bible is its name-o.
(Clap, clap, clap, clap, clap), (Clap, clap, clap, clap, clap),(Clap, clap, clap, clap, clap),
The Bible is its name-o.

SS1818

GAMES
WATER BALLOON VERSE GAME

Group children into pairs. Teach the children a short verse you would like them to know. Practice it over and over with them. Then let them practice it with their partners. Put two long pieces of string on the ground, parallel to each other, and about three feet apart. Have partners stand across from each other, one behind each string. Line all the children up behind the string and across from their partners. Give all the children behind the first string a small, water-filled balloon. The partners on one end start. The child with the balloon says the first word of the verse and then tosses the balloon to his/her partner. The next player says the second word and tosses the balloon. Play continues in this way. The person tossing the balloon may not step across the string, but the person catching it may step across the string after the balloon has been tossed. If a balloon lands on the ground and does not break, the same player must toss it again. Whenever a balloon breaks or whenever the partners can't correctly name the next word of the verse, they are out of the game. After each round, move the strings farther apart. Use the same verse or a different one. The last set of partners left are the winners.

JACOB'S COLOR STOMP

This is a good game to play after reading about the rainbow or about Joseph's coat of many colors. Divide the children into teams. Give all the members on one team balloons of the same color. Use a different color for each team. Each child ties a piece of yarn to the balloon and then ties it around his/her ankle. Children try to stomp on the balloons of other teams. A child is out of the game when his/her balloon is broken or when he/she leaves the designated boundaries. Boundaries can be marked with yarn. When there are only a few children left, the boundaries can be moved inward. The winning team is the last team to have someone left with a balloon.

"TWO BY TWO" GAMES

ACTIVITY SHEET "TWO BY TWO" GAME:

Look up the given verses to find the names of the animals listed. Write the verse reference next to the matching animal(s). You may use the same verse more than once. To win, be the first individual or team to find a pair of verses for each animal.

Genesis 1:24	Isaiah 11:6	Psalm 103:5	Matthew 7:15
Genesis 8:8	Luke 12:6	Joshua 11:4	Matthew 10:29
Genesis 12:16	Daniel 6:16	Leviticus 1:2	Matthew 3:16
Job 1:3	Jeremiah 13:23	Esther 6:8	Matthew 24:28

Wolf _____   _____

Sheep _____   _____

Leopard _____   _____

Lion _____   _____

Camel _____   _____

Horse _____   _____

Cattle _____   _____

Sparrows _____   _____

Eagles _____   _____

Dove _____   _____

OUTDOOR "TWO BY TWO" GAMES:

SACK RACE—Divide the group into pairs. Give a potato sack to each pair. Each child must put one leg into the sack and coordinate movements with his/her partner as they hop, walk, or run to the finish line. If they tear the sack, they are out. If there are a lot of children and only a few sacks, divide the children into heats.

WHEELBARROW RACE—One child in each pair lies face down on the ground. The other lifts the partner's legs and holds them up as he/she races on hands to the finish line.

ARM LINK RACE—Partners link arms at the elbow and race together to the finish line. Partners that become unlinked, must go back to start.

SS1818

ADAM AND EVE IN THE GARDEN

"ADAM AND EVE IN THE GARDEN" ACTIVITY SHEET GAME

You and one other player will each need a pencil and one of these sheets. Use the top grid. Write the letters A, D, A, and M (ADAM) horizontally or vertically in squares which are next to each other. Write the letters E, V, and E (EVE) in the same manner. Draw flowers in three of the remaining spaces. Your partner will be doing the same thing on his/her paper. When you are both ready, the first player names the letter and number of a square (D-2, for example). If the other player has something hidden in the square named, he/she must let the first player know by saying, "You found Adam," "You found Eve," or "You found a flower." If nothing is hidden in the square, he/she says, "You missed." Use the bottom grid to record your guesses. If you hit something, put a "+" in the square. If you miss, put a "–". Players take turns guessing squares. The first player to get 10 "+" signs on his/her guessing grid will have found all four letters of Adam, all three letters of Eve, and the three flowers. That player is the winner.

SS1818

"ADAM AND EVE IN THE GARDEN" OUTDOOR GAME

Laminate and cut out Adam and Eve. Use glue or rubber bands to attach them to a small box or plastic bottle. This will keep the wind from blowing them away outside. Divide the children into two teams, Adam's Team and Eve's Team. Choose someone from Adam's team to hide Adam. Choose someone from Eve's Team to hide Eve. The two players then sit out of the game. The rest of the players from the two teams must not watch as the figures are being hidden. All the players from Adam's Team look for Eve. All the players from Eve's Team look for Adam. If Adam is found first, Eve's team gets a point. If Eve is found first, Adam's team gets a point. Choose different children to hide Adam and Eve each round. The team with the most points after a set number of rounds wins.

SS1818

PICNIC PAIRS

Take this game along on a picnic and play it after you eat.

MATERIALS:

Two copies of this page per child (reproduced on tagboard, if possible)
Tagboard
Glue
Crayons or markers
Scissors

DIRECTIONS:

1. Color the pictures.
2. Cut out the cards. (Make the pieces sturdier by gluing them to tagboard before cutting if the cards have been reproduced onto regular paper instead of on tagboard. This way you will not be able to see through the cards when they are face down.)
3. Mix up the cards and place them face down in rows.
4. Find another child or two to play this memory game with you.
5. The first player turns two cards over. If the cards match, the player keeps them and gets another turn. If they don't match, it is the next player's turn. The winner is the player with the most matches after all the cards have been used.
6. If desired, the cards can be stored in the picnic basket on page 20.

SS1818

VERSE MYSTERY PUZZLE

The puzzle pieces below fit together to form a mystery shape.

MATERIALS:
Pattern
Scissors
Bible

DIRECTIONS:
1. Carefully cut out the pieces.
2. Try to put the puzzle together. You may want to have a race against other children.
3. If you need to, use your Bible to look up the verses given for clues to the mystery shape.

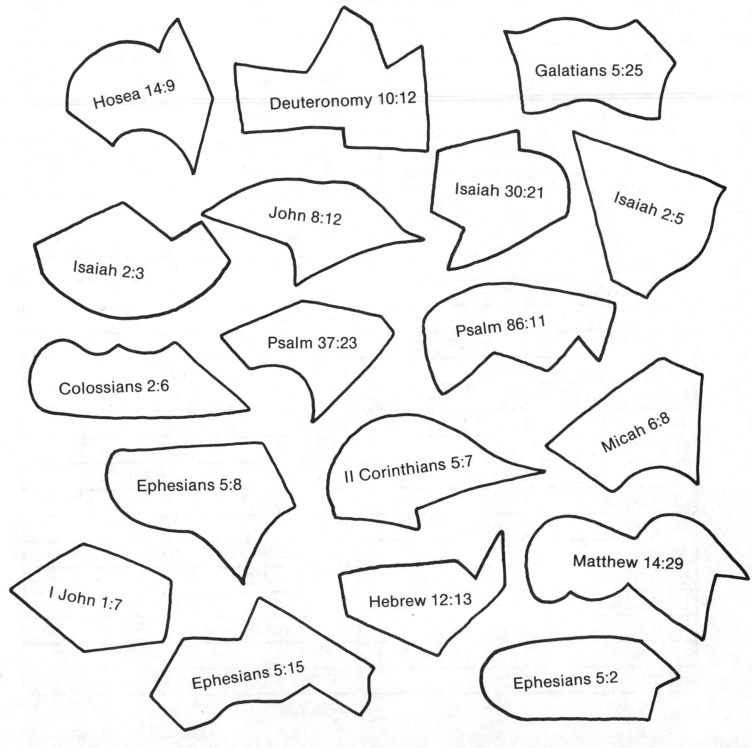

BIBLE BALL GAME

OUTDOOR BIBLE BALL GAME

Cut out the slips of paper which have the books of the Bible written on them. Put them in a bag. Set four bases in the shape of a diamond (just like in baseball) on a playing field. Put a ball that is good for kicking on or next to home plate. (There is no pitcher in this game.) Divide the children into two teams. One team lines up near home plate and the other spreads out on the field. The first player on the team lined up near home plate reaches into the bag and pulls out a slip of paper. He reads it out loud and tells whether the book written on it can be found in the Old Testament or the New Testament. A teacher or child tells the player whether or not the answer is correct. (A Bible can be used for reference.) The player returns the slip to the bag. If the player is incorrect, the team receives an out. If the player is correct, he or she kicks the ball and runs around the bases as far as he or she dares. If someone on the fielding team catches the ball before it touches the ground, the team receives an out. If someone on the fielding team hits a runner with a ball, the player is out unless he or she is touching a base. Once a player is out or safe, the ball is returned to home plate. (There is no stealing of bases.) Players take turns choosing a Bible slip and kicking the ball. Players on base may run only when a ball is kicked and not caught in the air. A player who reaches home safely, scores a point for his team. After three outs (or any number you decide), the fielding and kicking teams change places. Play as many rounds (innings) as you want.

GENESIS	EXODUS	LEVITICUS	NUMBERS
DEUTERONOMY	JOSHUA	JUDGES	RUTH
I SAMUEL	II SAMUEL	I KINGS	II KINGS
I CHRONICLES	II CHRONICLES	EZRA	NEHEMIAH
ESTHER	JOB	PSALMS	PROVERBS
ECCLESIASTES	SONG OF SOLOMON		ISAIAH
JEREMIAH	LAMENTATIONS	EZEKIEL	DANIEL
HOSEA	JOEL	AMOS	OBADIAH
JONAH	MICAH	NAHUM	HABAKKUK
ZEPHANIAH	HAGGAI	ZECHARIAH	MALACHI
MATTHEW	MARK	LUKE	JOHN
ACTS	ROMANS	I CORINTHIANS	II CORINTHIANS
GALATIANS	EPHESIANS	PHILIPPIANS	COLOSSIANS
I THESSALONIANS	II THESSALONIANS	I TIMOTHY	II TIMOTHY
TITUS	PHILEMON	HEBREWS	JAMES
I PETER	II PETER	I JOHN	II JOHN
III JOHN	JUDE	REVELATION	

Shining Star Publications, Copyright © 1990, A division of Good Apple, Inc.

SS1818

INDOOR BIBLE BALL GAME

You can play this game with a partner. Cut out the slips of paper containing the books of the Bible on page 74 and put them in a paper bag. Cut out the rectangles (biblical teammates) at the bottom of the page. These will be used as markers. You will need the biblical teammates from one team and your partner will need the biblical teammates from the other team. Roll a die to decide who will go first. The first player picks a slip from the bag. He tells whether it is an Old Testament book or a New Testament book. Use the table of contents in the Bible to verify answers. If incorrect, the player has an out. If correct, the player rolls the die and moves a biblical teammate around the bases according to the number rolled. A *one* means the "batter" and anyone on base can be moved one base, a *two* means they can be moved two bases, a *three* means they can be moved three bases, and a *four* means they can be moved four bases. *Five* and *six* count as outs. The same player keeps choosing slips and rolling the die until he gets three outs. Then it is the other player's turn. Whenever a biblical teammate reaches home, a point is scored. Play as many innings as you want. This is a good Bible game to take on summer vacations.

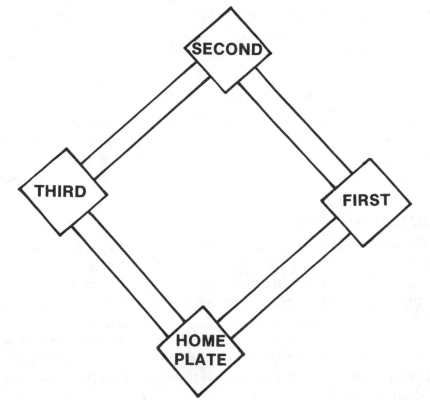

OLD TESTAMENT TEAM

Esther	Ruth	Samson	Joseph

NEW TESTAMENT TEAM

John	Zacchaeus	Martha	Peter

SS1818

SHEEP GAMES

FLOCK OF SHEEP

Divide the children into teams of about five players each. Have the children sit back to back in a circle, with elbows interlocked with the teammates next to them. At the signal, teams must attempt to stand together as a "flock" and move together to the finish line fifty feet away. If any elbows become "unlocked" at any time, the team must go back to start, sit back to back, and start over. The first flock to cross the finish line wins.

LAME SHEEP

Check the ground carefully before playing this game. Make sure it is free of glass, ant mounds, sharp stones, etc. Each child takes off one shoe and puts it on a pile with the shoes of all the other players. Mix up the shoes. Divide the players into two or three teams and have them form team lines about twenty feet away from the pile of shoes. At the signal, the first player (lame sheep) on each team hops on one foot (the foot with the shoe) to the pile. There, the player puts on his or her own shoe, and runs back to the team to touch the next player in line. The next player takes a turn. If a player puts down his shoeless (lame) foot on the way to the pile, he/she must run back to the end of his/her team's line to "rest" until his/her turn comes up again. The winning team is the first to have all players back at the starting line wearing shoes.

"LOST SHEEP" PAPER AND PENCIL GAME

Give teams or individuals ten minutes to search through the Bible for verses containing the word *sheep* or *lamb*. Players must write down the book, chapter, and verse number for each sheep or lamb found. The winner is the team or player who has found the most "lost" sheep and lambs at the end of the time period. You will have to verify the winning list.

"LOST SHEEP" OUTDOOR GAME

Hide 99 pieces of cotton and one cotton covered paper sheep. You can copy the one below and glue cotton to it. Hide the paper sheep in the most difficult place. Divide students into teams and give each team a paper bag. Let children look for the cotton balls and the special sheep. Any found can be put in the team's bag. The paper sheep counts as five points. The cotton balls are one point each. The team with the most points at the end of a given time period is the winner. Children might enjoy hiding the cotton balls and the sheep and inviting a younger class to find them. Older children might also like reading or acting out the story of the Lost Sheep (Luke 15:4-7 and Matthew 18:11-14) for the younger children.

Shining Star Publications, Copyright © 1990, A division of Good Apple, Inc.

SS1818

ANIMAL TAIL TAG

Divide children into groups of three or four with hands on the waist of the person in front of them. The last person on each team tucks a scarf or handkerchief "tail" near his/her waistline. All tails should be the same length. The entire team animal (lion, sheep, camel, or whatever goes along with a Bible story recently covered) must stay attached and must stay within given boundaries. The person at the front of the animal must try to grab the tails of the other animals. Teams which lose their tails, break apart, or go out of bounds are out. The last team left is the winner.

TOWER OF BABEL RELAY

Divide children into two teams. You will need the same number and the same kind of stackable objects (blocks, boxes, empty containers, etc.) for each team. Teams line up about twenty feet from their stacking materials. The first player stacks one of the objects on top of another, runs back to the starting line, tags the next player, and goes to the end of the line. Players take turns stacking an object onto the tower. If a player knocks down the tower, he must leave the objects as they are and return to the end of the line. The next player may restack one object. The game continues until one team has completed their "Tower of Babel."

SS1818

OLD TESTAMENT WHO'S WHO

ACTIVITY SHEET GAME

You will need to race through your Bible to find the person who matches the clue and verse reference. Write your answers on the lines. The first person or team to complete the answers correctly is the winner.

_____ A shepherd who was killed by his brother Cain (Genesis 4)

_____ The brother of Moses who spoke for him to the Pharaoh (Exodus 7)

_____ The "father" of many nations, blessed with a son in old age (Genesis 17)

_____ A man thrown into a lion's den (Daniel 6)

_____ A youth who fought Goliath (1 Samuel 17)

_____ Woman who encouraged a general to fight a battle which ended in victory (Judges 4)

_____ A prophet who was taken up by a whirlwind (II Kings 2)

_____ Brother of Jacob who was tricked out of a special blessing (Genesis 27)

_____ A queen who discovered Haman's plot to kill the Jews (Esther 7)

_____ Leader who surprised the enemies with pitchers, torches, and trumpets (Judges 7)

_____ A giant Philistine who was killed by a stone (I Samuel 17)

_____ Servant who was shown a well by an angel (Genesis 21)

_____ Noah's second son (Genesis 6)

_____ Son of Abraham (Genesis 21)

_____ A man who dreamed of a ladder reaching to heaven (Genesis 28)

_____ Man who warned the people of Nineveh to change their ways (Jonah 3)

_____ Wife of Jacob and mother of Joseph (Genesis 30)

_____ Wife of Isaac and the mother of twins (Genesis 27)

_____ King famous for his wisdom (I Kings 3)

· RUTH ·

INDOOR OR OUTDOOR GAME

Write Old Testament names on large cards. Each name must be different. Tie yarn to the cards so they can be worn around the players' necks. Players sit in a circle and wear a name tag. Practice pronouncing all the Old Testament names with the children. To play the game, each player slaps his or her knees with both hands, slaps them again, snaps the fingers of the right hand, and then snaps the fingers of the left hand. This sequence and rhythm is repeated and maintained throughout the game. A player is chosen to begin. Everyone keeps the rhythm, but the player chosen to begin calls out his own Old Testament name on the right-hand snap of fingers and another player's Old Testament name on the left-hand snap. The next chosen player calls out his own Old Testament name on the next right-hand snap and another player's Old Testament name on the next left-hand snap of fingers. Anyone who makes a mistake (such as not saying the right name on a snap or saying a name when he shouldn't) is out of the game and must leave the circle. Whenever someone misses, each remaining player removes his name tag and passes it to the player on his left. The player to the left of the player who missed starts the new round. The last player left is the winner.

Shining Star Publications, Copyright © 1990, A division of Good Apple, Inc.

SS1818

SUMMER WORD GAMES

". . . earth is full of the goodness of the Lord."   Psalm 33:5

ACTIVITY SHEET GAME

Fill in the chart with words beginning with E,A,R,T, and H for each category given. The winning team or individual is the first to finish or the one with the most spaces filled in correctly at the end of a ten-minute time period.

	E	A	R	T	H
FLOWER					
TREE					
BIRD					
FRUIT					
MAMMAL					

OUTDOOR OR INDOOR GAME

Give each child a Bible. Divide the class into 2 or 3 teams. Separate the children so that they can't see any other Bible, not even the Bible of a teammate. The teacher mentions something outside (grass, stone, flower, sky, etc.). The children have two minutes to search through the Bible to find the word and show it to the teacher. Each child who finds the word stays near the teacher until the end of the round and scores a point for his team. Decide ahead of time how many rounds will be played. The team with the most points at the end wins. A nature sticker or bookmark might be a good prize.

 SS1818

ALPHA-BIBLICAL ORDER GAMES

ACTIVITY SHEET GAME

Divide the children into teams. Each team will need a pencil and a copy of the list below. The first team to correctly unscramble all of the Bible words wins. The beginning letter is given for each word.

BARHAMA   A _Braham_

RAGEBG   B_eggar_

HAIRCOT   C_hariot_

ISPILEDC   D_isciple_

GALEE   E_agle_

CRANFUE   F _____

SINGEES   G_enesis_

REBH   H_erb_

LODI   I_Dol_

HOPSEJ   J_oesph_

GNIK   K_ing_

TINGILGHN   L_ight_

HARMAT   M_____

LEDEEN   N _____

TONIMENT   O_intment_

HARPHOA   P_haroah_

UEQEN   Q_ueen_

LEHCAR   R _____

ASMARTINA   S_amar_

PETLEM   T_emple_

CLEUN   U_nclean_

GAINREV   V _____

WEHAT   W_heat_

REXXES   X _____

KOYE   Y_oke_

CAASUZECH   Z _____

OUTDOOR GAME

Have children sit in a circle. Toss a beanbag or ball to a child. He/She must name a person, place, or thing mentioned in the Bible, which starts with *A*. Then the player must toss the beanbag or ball to another player who must think of a word for *B*. This continues for the entire alphabet. Players unable to give a correct answer within 20 seconds are out and must leave the circle. Players who answer correctly must cross their arms to indicate they had a successful turn. Other players should not toss the beanbag or ball to players with crossed arms. After everyone has had a turn, players remaining in the circle unfold their arms for a second round. Play continues with the next letter. Continue over and over again through the alphabet until only one player, the winner, remains.

SS1818

MY CUP RUNNETH OVER

ACTIVITY SHEET GAME

Psalm 23 below is overflowing with 23 extra words. Compare it with Psalm 23 in your Bible. Find and circle the 23 extra words. The first person to find them all wins.

The Lord is my good shepherd; I shall not want for anything.

He maketh me to lie down quietly in soft, green pastures: he leadeth me beside the still spring waters.

He restoreth my soul daily: he leadeth me always in the paths of righteousness for his name's sake.

Yea, though I walk swiftly through the low valley of the shadow of death, I will fear no evil: for thou art with me; my Lord; thy rod and thy staff they comfort me in time of need.

Thou preparest a fine table before me in the presence of mine enemies: thou anointest my head and my feet with oil; my cup runneth over.

Surely goodness and mercy shall follow me all the days of my life: and I will dwell in the heavenly house of the Lord for ever and ever.

OUTDOOR GAME

Divide children into two teams. Line the two teams up behind a large tub of water. Place two buckets, one for each team, about twenty-five feet away. Give the first player on each team a small plastic cup. On "go," the first child on each team dips the cup into the tub, fills it with as much water as he dares, and places it on top of his head. He holds the cup on his head and walks as quickly as possible toward his team's bucket. He tilts his head so that the water falls into the container. He keeps holding the cup on his head and rushes back to his team. He passes the cup to the next player and goes to the end of the line. The next player takes a turn. The winning team is the one to fill its container first or the one to have the most water in it at the end of a set time period.

SS1818

COLOR FUN

ACTIVITY SHEET COLOR FUN

Look up these verses to find a color word mentioned in each. Write the color on each line. You may want to race against other individuals or teams. Try to be the first to correctly complete the list.

1. Ecclesiastes 5:10 _____

2. Psalm 19:10 _____

3. Proverbs 23:31 _____

4. Psalm 23:2 _____

5. Revelation 3:4 _____

6. Proverbs 20:29 _____

7. Joshua 2:18 _____

8. John 4:35 _____

9. Luke 16:19 _____

10. Matthew 16:2 _____

OUTDOOR COLOR FUN

You will need four sheets of construction paper of different colors. Cut each into twenty or thirty squares. Put the squares, according to color, in four open boxes. Divide the children into team lines and assign each team one of the colors. Put a large bucket or box about twenty feet away from the team lines. Give each child a straw. The first player on each team bends over the team box and sucks on the straw to pick up a colored square. The player may not touch a square with his hands. He continues to suck on the straw as he runs to the large bucket or box which is about twenty feet away. If the paper falls off the straw, the player must use the straw to pick it up wherever it lands. The player may then continue toward the bucket. After depositing a square, the player runs back to the line and touches the next person on the team. The player then goes to the end of the line to await another turn. The game continues until one team has deposited all the team's squares in the large container.

SS1818

BIBLICAL TREASURE HUNTS

ACTIVITY SHEET TREASURE HUNT

Hunt through your Bible. Circle the ten verses which contain treasures such as gold, silver, coins, pearls, etc. The person or team finding the ten correct verses first is the winner.

Matthew 13:46
Luke 17:4
Mark 4:14
Psalm 35:27
Judges 5:3
I Kings 15:1
Psalm 118:1

Zechariah 9:16
I John 4:8
Luke 21:2
I Kings 10:29
Matthew 25:45
John 8:23
Psalm 119:72

I Kings 8:61
Matthew 26:15
II Timothy 2:20
Matthew 13:44
Proverbs 25:4
Luke 15:8

OUTDOOR TREASURE HUNT

Hide mites (pennies), pearls (marbles), or other treasures. The person or team finding the most objects wins. You can collect the treasures or let the children keep them as prizes.

OUTDOOR BIBLICAL WORD HUNT

Divide children into three teams. Give each team some Bibles and copies of one of the lists below. Each team will need a different list. You will need to hide the following items outdoors. For Team 1, hide a package of seeds, clay, a candle, a bottle, and a bowl. For Team 2, hide a book, keys, a toy camel, a paper crown, and some bread. For Team 3, hide a cup, an egg, a toy serpent, a toy lamb, and a cymbal. (Make paper substitutions if necessary.) Children look up the verses on their team's list. Then they try to find objects mentioned in the verses. The first team to find the five objects corresponding to the team's list is the winner.

TEAM 1
Psalm 126:6
Isaiah 64:8
Matthew 5:15
Mark 2:22
Ecclesiastes 12:6

TEAM 2
Isaiah 30:8
Matthew 16:19
Genesis 24:14
II Timothy 4:8
Proverbs 28:19

TEAM 3
Psalm 23:5
Job 6:6
Genesis 3:4
John 21:15
I Corinthians 13:1

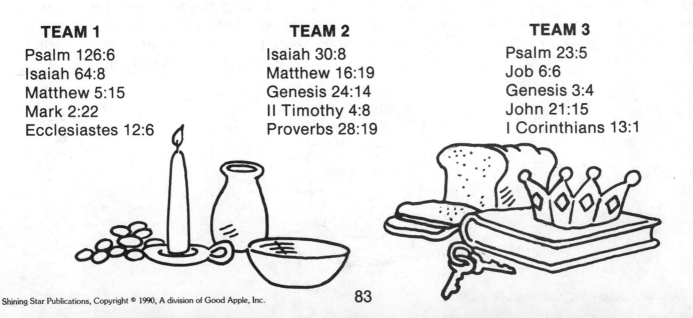

PLANTING SEEDS

These activities are good to use after studying growth, change, or parables about planting.

PLANTING GAME

Divide children into team lines of 4-6 players each. Each team will need a cup with twelve seeds, beans, or peanuts. Each team member will need a plastic spoon. Place the bottom portion of an empty egg carton (one per team) about fifteen feet away from the lines of children. On "go," the first player on each team reaches into the cup, pulls out a seed, and places it on the spoon. Then he races to the egg carton with the spoon in his mouth. He tilts the spoon with his mouth and "plants" a seed into one of the empty egg carton sections. Then he runs back and touches the next player on his team, who takes a turn. If a player touches a spoon with his hands or drops a seed, he must return to start. If he deposits a seed into one of the sections that already contains a seed, he must take it out and return to start. The winning team is the first one to get all twelve seeds planted.

A REAL PLANTING

Ask church personnel if they want any trees, vegetables, or flowers planted on the grounds. Ask permission, because someone will need to take care of the plants after Vacation Bible School is over. Be sure to plant something which can be planted in your area during the summer. This may limit the possibilities. Your planting can serve as a beautification project. If fruit trees, vegetables, or other plants which yield food are planted, the church members may want to use this as a service project to feed the hungry.

A SMALL PLANTING

Stuff cotton into a small paper cup. Out of a sponge, cut a circle just large enough to fit tightly inside the top of the cup. Soak the sponge in water and then set it on top of the cotton. Sprinkle dill, watercress, grass, or mustard seed on top of the wet sponge. Set the cup where it can get sunlight, but not in a place where the sponge will dry out too quickly. Your seeds will start to grow in about three days if you remember to keep the sponge moist at all times. You may want to draw a picture of Samson's head on the paper cup. Watch to see which "Samson" grows the longest "hair."

SS1818

CARNIVAL
HAVING A CARNIVAL

A carnival is a great event for the end of summer vacation or for the last day of Vacation Bible School! The carnival can be used as a fund-raiser, a service project, or just for fun.

1. First read through the explanations for carnival games given on the following pages. Decide which ones to use and get all materials needed or assign children to bring in specific materials.

2. Prior to carnival day, assign groups of children or classes of children to be in charge of each game. (If possible, also ask for adult volunteers to help with each game.) Children can help to color and cut out game pieces. They can also make signs on poster board depicting the game titles. (optional)

3. A work schedule will be needed for each game. A few children at a time will be needed to "work" at each carnival game. (You may also want to schedule an adult volunteer for each game to make sure things run smoothly.) Children may switch off at regular intervals. This allows them time to play all the games and time to "work" the game they've been assigned. All children are responsible for game and grounds cleanup at the end of the carnival.

4. Make several copies of the win tickets found on the next page. The number of copies needed will depend on the number of people who will be playing the carnival games. Children can color and cut out the tickets. They can sort the tickets by title into boxes or bags for each game. On each box or bag, write "WIN TICKETS." You will need a second box or bag for each game. On this one, tape a copy of the game directions. These can be referred to on the day of the carnival. Label the second box or bag "PLAY TICKETS."

5. Buy or make some tickets which can be used by the children to play games. Call these play tickets. Decide on the purpose of the carnival. If the carnival is to be just for fun, give each child an equal number of tickets on the day of the carnival and let the children use them to play whatever games they wish. If the carnival is to be used as a fund-raiser or as a service project, you will need to have adults selling the tickets on the day of the carnival. (You will need to have plenty of change on hand in such a case.) Proceeds can go toward Vacation Bible School expenses or can be donated to a needy family or organization.

6. Children need to know how to work at the game they've been assigned. Explain the directions and the work schedule. Tell them to collect a play ticket from each player and to put it in the bag or box labeled "PLAY TICKETS." If a player wins, they can give him one or two win tickets according to the game directions.

7. Decide whether drinks, popcorn, baked goods, or other snacks are to be served or sold on carnival day. Get all necessary items and volunteers to make and distribute them.

8. Decide who is to be invited to Carnival Day. You may want just Vacation Bible School children, or you may wish to include their friends and relatives. You may even want to announce the carnival in a church bulletin and have it open to all members of the church family. If the carnival is to be in your backyard, you may want to invite friends and relatives. You may even want to use some of the games at a birthday party. In any case, you may need flyers, posters, or printed announcements. Be sure to include the date, time, something about the carnival, etc.

9. Obtain prizes such as summer bookmarks, toy animals, Frisbees, jump ropes, baseballs, etc. On the day of the carnival, display the prizes and the ticket values. Children can trade win tickets for prizes. A bookmark might be worth 1 win ticket, while a baseball might be worth 15. A teacher or adult volunteer may be in charge of the prize table.

10. Select places to set up the games, tickets, snacks, and prizes. Many games can be set up on the ground, but you may need to set others on benches or tables. You may also need a few folding chairs for parent volunteers. On the day of the carnival, have children and parent volunteers set up any benches, tables, or chairs needed. Then have them set up game materials. Have the ticket boxes or bags ready for each game. (optional) Tape game signs to the tables or benches. Decorate game areas with paper streamers and balloons.

11. Let the games begin!

 SS1818

CARNIVAL WIN TICKETS

Give winners of each carnival game one or two of these tickets as indicated in the directions of each carnival game.

DANIEL'S LION GAME

WIDOW'S MITE TOSS

NOAH'S ARK TOSS

FISHERS OF MEN GAME

JONAH'S WHALE

LOST SHEEP GAME

CREATION GAME

RAINBOW GAME

DAVID'S STONE THROW

"WALK" ON WATER GAME

SS1818

DANIEL'S LION GAME

"DANIEL'S LION" ACTIVITY SHEET GAME

Play with a partner. Start with five paper clips, coins, or beans. (Some objects are more difficult to use than others, because they bounce or roll.) Stand five feet away from the target. Toss the five objects. Then add up your score. You may count anything completely or partially within the lion's mouth, eyes, or nose.

"DANIEL'S LION" OUTDOOR GAME AND CARNIVAL GAME

Enlarge the lion's head above (except for the numbers) onto a heavy piece of cardboard. Cut out holes for the mouth, eyes, and nose. Slant the cardboard against a weighed box and tape the top of the lion's head to the box. A player stands about eight feet away from the lion. (Younger children may stand closer.) The player needs three balls or beanbags (which can be made by tying a knot in a small sock filled with beans) to toss into the holes. Players who get one or two objects into the hole receive a "Daniel's Lion" win ticket. Players who toss all three objects into the holes receive two win tickets.

NOAH'S ARK TOSS

Make two copies. Color the animals. Laminate them, if possible. Then cut them out. Use rubber bands and/or paper clips to attach them to weighed cartons. Put a clothespin at the top of each carton and set the cartons in two rows. Make five rings to toss by cutting out sections of round ice-cream containers or other round containers. The player stands behind a line about six feet from the containers. The player tosses the five rings. If two or more land around any of the clothespins on the animal cartons, the player wins and is given a "Noah's Ark Toss" win ticket. If two rings land around the same clothespin or around the clothespins of containers containing the same kind of animal, the player gets two win tickets.

SS1818

JONAH'S WHALE OF A SPLASH SPONGE THROW

Try to obtain a large appliance box. Sketch a whale, like the one below, on one side of the box. Use filament tape to tape a heavy, clear piece of plastic (such as a shower curtain) over the whale. The plastic is not absolutely necessary, but it will keep the box from getting soggy if the game is used for a long length of time. Cut a hole the size of a person's face through the plastic and the box at the place indicated in the picture. Volunteers will be standing or sitting inside the box, so you will need to make sure they can get into the box through lid folds or a cut opening. Set plastic garbage bags in front of the whale so tossed sponges will remain fairly clean when they land. Set another garbage bag about twenty feet in front of the whale. Put two large buckets of water and about a dozen sponges on the garbage bag. Players dip three sponges into the water and toss them at the person in the whale opening. Any player who is able to splash the "whale" in the face with two out of the three sponges gets a "Whale of a Splash" win ticket. Game booth workers will need to refill one bucket at a time with clean water while the other bucket is in use. Switch whale volunteers at set intervals. Whale volunteers should be told ahead of time to bring a towel and to wear old clothes. They should not wear contacts or glasses.

NOTE: If a large box is not available, simply drape a volunteer in plastic, sit him on a chair, and hang a sign on him saying "Whale of a Good Sport" or "Jonah's Whale." Have the players toss sponges at his face.

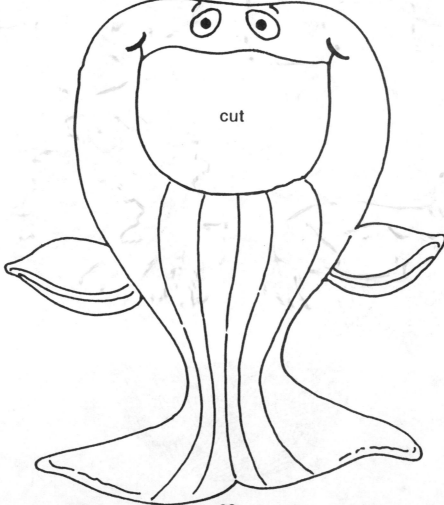

SS1818

CREATION GAME

On a large piece of cardboard, draw an enlarged version of the picture shown. If you have an overhead projector, you can enlarge each circle given. Then color, laminate, and stick to a piece of cardboard. The carnival player stands about six feet away and tosses three beanbags and then adds up the score. (Beanbags can be made by putting beans into a sock and then tying a knot in the sock.) Count any beanbag which is at least partially within a circle. If a player scores 6-12 points, he/she receives one "Creation Game" win ticket. Players scoring 13 or more points may receive two win tickets.

SS1818

DAVID'S STONE THROW

Get three large, empty detergent boxes. Enlarge the three pieces of Goliath below onto paper the size of the front of the detergent boxes. Color with crayons or markers and laminate, if possible. Tape the sections of Goliath to the three boxes. Stack the detergent boxes one on top of the other to form Goliath. Players start with five stones (just like David did). The stones can be soft, spongy balls, plastic balls, or beanbags. The player stands about twenty feet away from the stacked boxes and throws the stones. A player who can knock all three parts of Goliath down with his five stones receives a "David's Stone Toss" win ticket. A player who knocks all three parts down on the first throw receives two win tickets.

SS1818

WIDOW'S MITE TOSS

Luke 21:1-4 and Mark 12:41-44

"WIDOW'S MITE" ACTIVITY SHEET GAME

Play with a friend. Stand five feet away from this sheet. The first player "casts" pennies one at a time until two of them land completely inside the treasure box. Then it is the next player's turn. The winner is the player who gets two pennies in the box with the least amount of tries.

"WIDOW'S MITE" OUTDOOR GAME AND CARNIVAL GAME

Set up a collection plate, collection basket, or a shoe box "treasury." Players stand behind a line about eight feet away from the treasury. Players start with five coins, pebbles, beans, or other objects which are used to represent the widow's mites. Anyone who can toss two out of the five mites into the treasury is a winner. Carnival winners receive a "Widow's Mite" win ticket.

Shining Star Publications, Copyright © 1990, A division of Good Apple, Inc.

SS1818

FISHERS OF MEN

Make two or three copies of this page on heavy paper. Laminate and cut out the rectangles. Put a piece of magnetic tape on the back of each rectangle. Mix up the rectangles and place them face down, so the magnets are facing up. Tie a horseshoe magnet to a piece of string. Tie the other end of the string to a dowel rod, stick, or unsharpened pencil. The game player holds onto the "fishing rod" and tries to catch a rectangle. Once a rectangle is caught, it is checked to see whether it is a man or a fish. A player who catches a man is a winner. He receives a "Fishers of Men Game" win ticket.

SS1818

RAINBOW GAME

Use the rainbow below, or make a larger one on a piece of poster board. Color the stripes red, orange, yellow, green, blue, and violet. (Use only six colors, because there are only six sides on a die.) The player puts a marker on any of the numbered colored arches. Then he/she rolls the die. If the number on the die matches the number on the colored arch, the player gets a "Rainbow Game" win ticket.

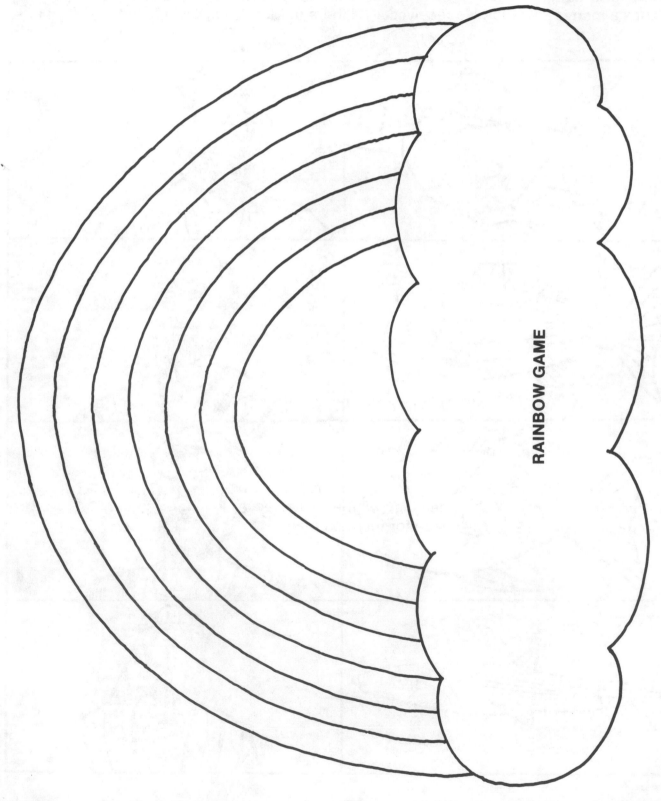

RAINBOW GAME

SS1818

"WALK" ON WATER GAME

Cut off the top few inches of a few large paper milk cartons. Fill them about three-fourths full of water. Arrange the cartons a few inches apart. The player stands about five feet away from the cartons and tosses three ping pong balls at them. If one or two of the balls land on the water, the player receives a "Walk on Water Game" win ticket. If all three Ping-Pong balls land on the water, the players receives two win tickets.

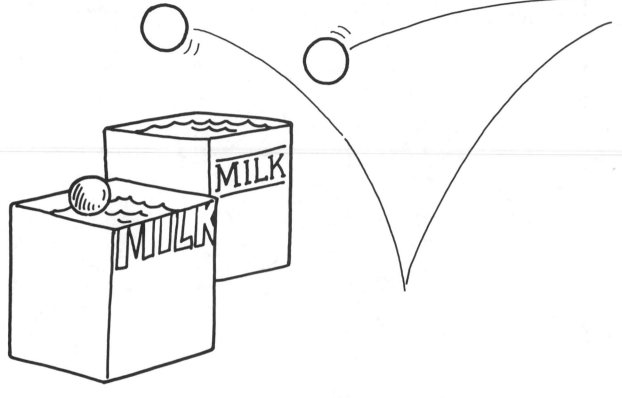

LOST SHEEP

On a table or cardboard box, set twelve paper cups upside down. If desired, the cups may be decorated with paper bushes, rocks, trees, etc. to signify hiding places for the sheep. Hide a "sheep" (piece of cotton) under one of the cups. A player may lift three cups. If the lost sheep is under one of them, he receives a "Lost Sheep" win ticket. Hide the sheep in a different place for the next player.

ANSWER KEY

"TWO BY TWO" GAME, Page 69

Wolf—Isaiah 11:6 and Matthew 7:15
Sheep—Genesis 12:16; Job 1:3 and Matthew 7:15
Leopard—Isaiah 11:6 and Jeremiah 13:23
Lion—Isaiah 11:6 and Daniel 6:16
Camel—Genesis 12:16 and Job 1:3

Horse—Joshua 11:4 and Esther 6:8
Cattle—Genesis 1:24 and Leviticus 1:2
Sparrows—Matthew 10:29 and Luke 12:6
Eagle—Matthew 24:28 and Psalm 103:5
Dove—Genesis 8:8 and Matthew 3:16

VERSE MYSTERY PUZZLE, Page 73

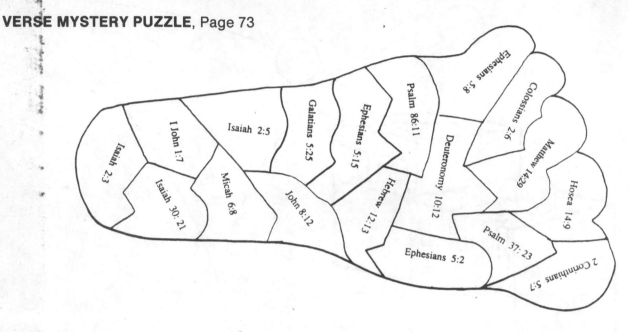

OLD TESTAMENT WHO'S WHO, Page 78

Abel, Aaron, Abraham, Daniel, David, Deborah, Elijah, Esau, Esther, Gideon, Goliath, Hagar, Ham, Issac, Jacob, Jonah, Rachel, Rebekah, Solomon

ALPHA-BIBLICAL ORDER GAME, Page 80

Abraham, beggar, chariot, disciple, eagle, furnace, Genesis, herb, idol, Joseph, king, lightning, Martha, needle, ointment, Pharaoh, queen, Rachel, Samaritan, temple, uncle, vinegar, wheat, xerxes, yoke, and Zacchaeus

MY CUP RUNNETH OVER, Page 81

Extra words are: good, for, anything, quietly, soft, spring, daily, always, swiftly, low, my, Lord, in time, of, need, fine, and, my, feet, heavenly, and ever

COLOR FUN GAMES, Page 82

1. silver, 2. gold, 3. red, 4. green, 5. white, 6. gray, 7. scarlet, 8. white, 9. purple, 10. red

BIBLICAL TRASURE HUNT, Page 83

Matthew 13:46, Psalm 119:72, Zechariah 9:16, Luke 21:2, I Kings 10:29, Matthew 26:15, II Timothy 2:20, Matthew 13:44, Proverbs 25:4, and Luke 15:8

SS1818